There's No Lake on Lake Street!

THERE'S NO LAKE ON LAKE STREET!

COLORFUL ORIGINS OF STREET AND PLACE NAMES IN RENO, SPARKS, CARSON CITY, AND SOUTH SHORE LAKE TAHOE

JAMES D. UMBACH

There's No Lake on Lake Street! Colorful Origins of Street and Place Names in Reno, Sparks, Carson City, and South Shore Lake Tahoe. Copyright © 2013 James D. Umbach.

Published by
Umbach Consulting & Publishing
6966 Sunrise Blvd., #263
Citrus Heights, CA 95610
916-733-2159
ken@umbachconsulting.com

ISBN: 978-1-937123-07-9

Library of Congress Control Number: 2013905299

Photos at start of Reno, Carson City, and South Lake Tahoe sections are from the Library of Congress American Memory Collection, with no known usage restrictions. Photo at start of Sparks section is from the Robert Mitchell Elementary School website, and believed to be in the public domain.

Cover design by Shawn Hansen, SHMarketingSolutions.com.

Front cover photos/images, used by permission:

       "Field of Wheat" © Dan Breckwoldt

       "Man with Map" © Gualtiero Boffi

       "Blank Traffic Signs" © Olga D. Van De Veer

       "Blank Green Traffic Sign" © Shahorohani

Contents

DEDICATION

To my parents, who always said I had a book in me. Well, here it is.

And, to the family members who passed away during the writing of this book:

Ruth Shelton

Margaret Clopine-Ikerman

George Wells, Jr.

Reginald H. (Reggie) Rowland

ACKNOWLEDGMENTS

First of all, I would like to thank my parents, who encouraged the reading bug early on—at the age of three. Reading, of course, leads to writing, and writing leads to books. Special thanks to my father, for helping get this book into your hands, and with providing the tools with which to do it. I couldn't have done it without him.

Thanks go my wife, of course, for putting up with my hogging the computer to "work on writing." Of course, the secret is that I wasn't always writing this book—sometimes my research would lead me off in another direction, and I'd end up gathering material for a future book. (Don't tell her that.)

Special recognition goes to my co-workers at John Ascuaga's Nugget in Sparks, who often asked me questions that ended up getting answered in this book. Your encouragement kept me going.

I'd like to give a special shout out to the staff at the Washoe County Library's Downtown Reno branch, for helping point me in the proper direction when my research hit a dead end at times.

I don't know if it's proper to thank pets, as well, but the truth is that our cockatiels, Tia and Rio, helped provide me companionship by perching on my shoulder (or occasionally on my head) during those early morning writing spells when the rest of the family was asleep. (Tia, I am sorry to report, passed away in the summer of 2011.)

RENO

Overhead View of Reno, 1908

By way of introduction to Reno, here is an excerpt from *Harper's Magazine*, June 1925. More of these "sidebars" will appear throughout the book.

Reno, 1925.

That is the happy city Reno would, in her heart of hearts, like to be—not a Port Sunlight or a Spotless Town or a Brookline, Massachusetts, or a Los Angeles, California. It is reduced instead to being a divorce mart and to finding its romance in its scenery—as the divorcées apparently are reduced to being "aces in the hole" for the males so vividly characterized by my young friend. Being Western—though Nevadan—it does its civic duty in the matter of planting trees, making wide streets, erecting beautiful school buildings. Its provision for public entertainment is small—smaller than that made by most isolated American towns. I never quite got over wondering why. Probably, however, you must go into the recesses of the Nevadan heart to find any answer. You do not take trouble to provide yourself (or the stranger within your gates) with amusement that does not amuse you. Horse racing amuses them—and they have the meetings of the Silver State Jockey Club. Prize fights amuse them, and good liquor—but the laws are inconvenient, evade them as you will. Religion and chautauquas do not amuse them. Books and music and pictures and plays do not amuse them—and there are none. Because the eyes of the world are upon them they must be discreet—and Reno is, as we have said, a dull town for the law-abiding visitor. Even divorce does not amuse them much: it has merely come to be the most valuable local commodity. The civilized people make their own life after the fashion of their Western kind—with much dependence on the scenery and motor cars, and on simple outdoor pleasures. But the excitement they crave is not the excitement that women's clubs or church sociables or a municipal entertainment committee can give them. They do not put out their hands for such pleasures . . .

Curious little Reno! So pretty, so uneventful, so isolated—so very "small-town"—yet so manifestly linked to a brilliant and lawless past; and bearing for all eyes in the broad light of day the light flotsam of divorcées, the heavy jetsam of shifty, broken men.

(Katharine Fullerton Gerould, writing about Reno for *Harper's Magazine*, June 1925.)

Arlington Avenue

Combined in 1959 from two streets originally called Belmont and Chestnut. The street is named for the Arlington Ranch, which was land owned by Jane Lake, wife of the founder of Reno, Myron Lake.

Artemesia Way

Artemesia (correctly spelled Artemisia) is a type of daisy found throughout the arid climate of the North American deserts, among other places. Sagebrush, a species of Artemisia, is found throughout the Reno area, and even the entire state of Nevada, giving the state its nickname, the Sagebrush State. Sagebrush is known for its sweet smell.

Balzar Circle

This street is named for Frederick B. Balzar (1880–1934), Governor of Nevada from 1927 until his death in 1934. He was responsible for preventing "bank runs" of the 1930s within Nevada by calling for a moratorium on all banks in the state. However, his two most famous acts as Governor were to re-establish legal gaming in the state and to provide for a six-week residency requirement for divorce.

Before becoming Governor, he served as a conductor of the Carson & Colorado Railroad (running between Hawthorne, Nevada, and Keeler, California). He later served in both the State Assembly and the State Senate, and was Sheriff of Mineral County from 1917 to 1926.

Fred Balzar is the only governor of Nevada to have died in the Governor's Mansion.

Baker Street

Named for the Baker family, who had a stable in this area.

Bartley Ranch Road

Because of the new irrigation ditches in the area in the 1870s, the Truckee Meadows became a prime ranching area: alfalfa, cattle, and sheep. In 1912, an Italian immigrant, Demetrio Buscaglia, bought a ranch south of Reno. The land became a dairy, and later a horse boarding establishment. His son, Gus, changed his last name to the more pronounceable "Bartley" and went on to become a well known rodeo performer before selling the ranch to the county in 1988. See also Caughlin Ranch Boulevard.

Beaumont Parkway

Robert J. Beaumont once owned the land upon which the former Northgate Golf Course now sits. Beaumont deeded the land to the county for the public to enjoy, with the provision that the county design and build an 18-hole golf course on the site. That golf course operated until 2008, when it was closed due to budget constraints.

Beckwourth Drive

One of the few streets in Reno named for a black, this street honors James Beckwourth (1798–1867), who escaped a life of slavery and joined a trading/exploration party in the Rocky Mountains. He slowly worked his way west, joining the Crow tribe of Indians as a scout and interpreter. The Crow liked him so much that he was later named chief of their tribe!

But the real reason that people in California and Nevada remember Beckwourth today is for his discovery of the Sierra pass that now bears his name. At only about 5,200 feet in elevation, it is considerably lower than nearby Donner and Echo passes, and frequently remains open during storms that close the other two better-known routes. Therefore, because of Beckwourth, many people are able to travel over the mountain along California Highway 70 during the winter when the other options are blocked.

Some Recollections of James P. Beckwourth

I was destined to disappointment, for that same night Marysville was laid in ashes. The mayor of the ruined town congratulated me upon bringing a train [wagon, not locomotive] through [the new pass]. He expressed great delight at my good fortune, but regretted that their recent calamity had placed it entirely beyond his power to obtain for me any substantial reward. With the exception of some two hundred dollars subscribed by some liberal-minded citizens of Marysville, I received no indemnification for the money and labor I have expended upon my discovery. The city had been greatly benefited by it, as all must acknowledge, for the emigrants that now flock to Marysville would otherwise have gone to Sacramento. Sixteen hundred dollars I expended upon the road is forever gone, but those who derive advantage from this outlay and loss of time devote no thought to the discoverer; nor do I see clearly how I am to help myself, for every one knows I can not roll a mountain into the pass and shut it up.

But there is one thing certain: although I recognize no superior in love of country, and feel in all its force the obligation imposed upon me to advance her interests, still, when I go out hunting in the mountains a road for every body to pass through, and expending my time and capital upon an object from which I shall derive no benefit, it will be because I have nothing better to do.

(From *The Life and Adventures of James P. Beckwourth, Mountaineer, Scout, and Pioneer, and Chief of the Crow Nation of Indians, Written from his own Dictation*, by T. D. Bonner, 1856.)

For those interested in learning more about Jim Beckwourth, I strongly recommend a visit to the Plumas County Museum, about two hours east of Reno in the town of Quincy, California. En route, you can visit the old Beckwourth Cabin in Portola.

Bell Street

Bell street is named for Frank Bell (1840–1927), who acted as Nevada's Governor for four months in 1890, filling the term of Charles C. Stevenson, the state's first governor to die in office.

Before becoming governor, Bell supervised telegraph service in both California and Nevada, including lines from Placerville to Virginia City, the Overland Telegraph, and the Central Pacific's own line. He also was warden of the Nevada State Prison and was Reno's Justice of the Peace.

Upon Nevada's statehood in 1864, it was Frank Bell who tapped the telegram of the new state's Constitution to Washington, D.C. At the time, that was the longest telegram ever sent.

Bell declined to run for a full term as Governor, since his brother-in-law, Christopher C. Powning (developer of Powning's Addition, one of the first subdivisions in Reno), wanted to run for U.S. Senate, and Bell felt that both brothers running could interfere with each other's campaign.

Who is Governor?

CARSON, Sept. 25 – Considerable discussion is going on relative to who is now Governor of Nevada. Some hold that Frank Bell, being Lieutenant-Governor, becomes acting Governor by reason of the Governor's death, but owing to a Constitutional provision he cannot draw the salary. Others hold that Governor and Lieutenant-Governor, H.C. Davis, being dead, the President of the Senate takes the place. Others urge that Secretary of State

14

> Dormer is the party who really is Governor. Considerable trouble on this account and something of a mixed up state of affairs may be the result.
>
> (*San Francisco Call*, September 26, 1890.)

Berrum Lane

Named for Louis W. Berrum, who bought the nearby Moana Hot Springs Resort from its original developers in 1913, and sold it to the city as a recreational area in 1956. The city closed the facility in 2007. However, as of this writing plans are underway to redevelop it as a community sports complex with soccer and softball fields.

See also Moana Lane.

Bible Way

No, it has nothing to do with Scriptures or books. Instead, Bible Way is named for Alan Bible (1909–1988), a prominent 20th Century Reno figure. Bible is perhaps best known for being the catalyst for the Southern Nevada Water Project. After graduating from the University of Nevada, Reno, he served as the District Attorney for Storey County and, later, the Nevada Attorney General. Following the death of Sen. Pat McCarran, Bible was elected to the United States Senate in 1954, where he served until 1974.

Booth Street

Named for Reno High Teacher Libby, or "Libbie," Booth. See Libby Booth, in the Reno schools section.

California Avenue

This street got its name simply because it heads west from its intersection with Virginia Street, and if you continue walking west, you'll be in the state of California in just a few miles.

Cannan Way

Named for Rita Cannan, principal of Mary S. Doten school. See Rita Cannan, in the Reno schools section.

Carville Drive

Named in honor of Edward P. Carville (1885–1956), Governor of Nevada from 1939-1945. He was Deputy District Attorney of Elko County, then later a judge there. In 1934, he became the U.S. Attorney for Nevada before getting elected Governor in 1938. He resigned the office of Governor during his second term in order to become a United States Senator for Nevada in 1945, a position he held for only a few months before becoming a private attorney.

Cashill Boulevard

Named in honor of Bill Cashill (1914–1960). Born in New Jersey, he moved to Reno and attended Reno High and the University of Nevada, where he was a star football player and earned a degree in economics. He later went to Harvard for his law degree.

In 1940, he was elected to the State Assembly, and he became Speaker only one year later. His promising political career ended abruptly, however, when Cashill went into the Naval Reserve following the 1941 Pearl Harbor attack.

After the war, Cashill was a successful lawyer in Reno, and helped plan the 1960 Squaw Valley Winter Games.

Caughlin Ranch Boulevard

Named in honor of Crissie Andrews Caughlin, wife of Washoe County Sheriff William Caughlin. Her father, George Andrews, received the land as thanks for designing the canals that provided water to the ranches throughout the Truckee Meadows.

See also Bartley Ranch Road.

Chism Street

Chism Street is named for the Chism family, who once had a ranch in this area. The family ran a successful dairy and ice cream factory from the property from the 1900s until the 1950s. (In fact, they used a waterwheel in the Truckee River to provide power!) The original ranch house is still visible at 1401 West 2nd Street, near the railroad tracks, though it has been remodeled and expanded over the years. Later, the property became a successful "auto court" (the predecessor to what we would call a "motel" nowadays).

The house remains in the Chism family to this day. (Former mayor and city councilman John E. Chism was great-great-nephew of the original owner, Gardner Chism.)

Coliseum Way

Coliseum Way fronts what was originally the Centennial Coliseum, now known as the Reno-Sparks Convention Center. The Centennial Coliseum got its name because it opened in 1965, one hundred and one years after Nevada became a state.

Country Club Drive

This street honors the Reno Golf Club, built as Reno's first exclusive members-only country club. The club was founded in 1917 by Gourlay Dunn Webb, who arrived in Reno from England and was dismayed to find that her new hometown did not have any available golf facilities. Only nine years later, a major fire destroyed the clubhouse, but it was rebuilt shortly thereafter. However, the club never fully recovered from the fire, especially in the time of the Great Depression, and it closed its doors in 1933. The county realized the importance of recreation for its citizens, so it developed the land into the Washoe County Golf Course in 1936. Though the club it is named for is long gone, the street name remains.

Golf Club For Reno Is Plan. Mrs. Gourlay Dunn-Webb, English Instructor, Behind Movement; Her Plans Are Meeting With Success. Says This City Can Support First Class Club and She Has Picked Out Spot For Links; Many Assisting

Reno residents will soon be able to enjoy a few moments after business affairs at golf, if the efforts of Mrs. Gourlay Dunn-Webb, one of the country's best known golf experts, who is now in Reno, are successful.

Receives Encouragement

Mrs. Dunn-Webb has gained considerable fame as a golf teacher for women and she is bending every effort to organize a golf club here and said this morning that she was meeting with much encouragement.

"Reno should support a golf club and a good one too," said Mrs. Dunn-Webb this morning, "and I feel sure that my plans will be successful. I have taken to the proposition of organizing a club with several of the prominent residents of the city and they are all enthusiastic."

Came From England

Mrs. Dunn-Webb came to Reno from England about a month ago, where she gained fame both as a player and a teacher of golf. She is the only woman professional golf player in America. She came to this country from England and is descendant from a long line of noted golf players. Her first teaching was done in the Princess Golf Club of England near London, which is one of the principal golf clubs of England.

Her mother was a teacher of golf and her father, the late Thomas Dunn, was acknowledged the greatest golf teacher of his time. Her grandfather and great-grandfather were golf teachers of note. She has had considerable experience during her short stay in this country in managing golf clubs for women, besides teaching.

Has Links Located

Mrs. Dunn-Webb has made good use of the month she has been in Reno and has not only worked up considerable interest in the subject of starting a club but has located a place for a links that will "just fill the bill."

"The introduction of the 'royal and ancient' game into Reno would, I am sure, be very much welcomed," said Mrs. Dunn-Webb.

"When a golfer reaches a place where there is no golf course his first and most natural impulse is to make a place.

"Golf is a strangely fascinating game. It is not without good reason they call it the world game now. It has alighted upon every country and wherever it has touched it has seized. It is a game for both old and young. John D. Rockefeller, on his retirement from business, had a golf course made for him. He started the game when he was 66 years of age."

Should be Supported

"In a flourishing town like Reno a country golf club could be well supported. Golf is a modern necessity to the traveler."

Several attempts to start a golf club here in the past four or five years have failed but from the

19

support which is being given Mrs. Dunn-Webb's plans this move will be successful.

(From the *Reno Evening-Gazette*, January 5, 1917.)

Damonte Ranch Parkway

Louis Damonte owned several ranches in the area in the middle part of the 20th century. Damonte purchased the ranch in 1940 from the descendants of its original owner, Peleg Brown, who originally planned the ranch to be a stopover point for travelers heading between Reno, Tahoe, and Virginia City.

Dandini Boulevard

This winding, mountainous road leading to higher education is named for Count Alessandro Dandini (1899–1991). Dandini, a faculty member at the University of Nevada, Reno, helped secure the land for the placement of what is now the Desert Research Institute and Truckee Meadows Community College.

Dandini was also an inventor and held 22 patents. Among other inventions, we have him to thank for the three-way light bulb and the retractable automobile top.

Dickerson Road

Dickerson Road is named for Denver Dickerson (1872–1925) who was the Governor of Nevada from 1908 to 1911. Born in California, he was a miner in that state as well as Idaho and Montana before fighting in the Spanish-American War. After the war, he moved to Ely, Nevada, and became editor of the *White Pine News*.

In 1906, upon discovering that nobody was interested in running for Lieutenant Governor, Dickerson decided to run. He won the election, then became acting Governor following the death of John Sparks.

Dickerson was instrumental in bringing the 1910 Jeffries-Johnson bout (the most famous interracial boxing match) to Reno, despite much local and national opposition. The black pugilist, Jack Johnson, won and there was speculation that the fight was fixed. Many people believe that this fight is the main reason that Dickerson lost his bid for reelection.

After his term as Governor, Dickerson became superintendent of the Nevada State Police, then Warden of the State Prison in Carson City.

Nevada's Governor Slaps Editor's Face

CARSON CITY, Nev., Aug. 17 – Governor Denver S. Dickerson walked into the office of the Carson News last evening and, after talking a few minutes with Editor George Montrose, slapped Montrose in the face. Dickerson accused Montrose of printing an article in the News defamatory of the character of the chief executive. The article in question accused Dickerson of grafting in connection with the selection of the prison site.

(*San Francisco Call*, August 18, 1910.)

Double Diamond Boulevard

The modern, gleaming office buildings lining this area give no hint of the land's past as a ranch, owned by Wilbur May (1898–1982), son of David May, founder of the Mayco department store chain. Wilbur traveled the world collecting artifacts, many of which are now on display at the aptly named Wilbur May museum, located near the university in Rancho San Rafael Park. In 2006, Federated bought the remaining Mayco stores and converted them to Macy's.

The Double Diamond Ranch, by the way, was named for the graphic that results from stacking May's initials, one above the other.

Evans Avenue

Named for John Newton Evans (1835–1904), a cattle rancher and banker during Reno's early history. He is best known for selling to the state the property on which the University of Nevada now sits, so it could relocate the university from its then-home in Elko.

In the original plat of the city, Evans Street, of course, was not named as such. For several years, it was known as Peavine Street, after a prominent volcano northwest of the city.

Foster Drive

Foster Drive honors Herb Foster, a former football and basketball coach at Reno High School who later went on to become that school's athletic director. Foster died on Christmas Day in 1948, and when the school was moved to its current location in 1951, the school wanted to be sure to honor its beloved staff member.

Frandsen Circle

Named in honor of Peter Frandsen, a Danish biologist who graduated from the University of Nevada in 1895, then taught there for 40 years. The Frandsen Humanities Building on the campus is also named for him.

Fulton Alley

Named in honor of Robert L. Fulton (1847–1920), a prominent Reno citizen during the town's early days. He had a long career with the Erie Railroad in Ohio, serving first as a telegraph operator, then a conductor. Upon hearing about the plans to construct a railroad all the way to the Pacific Ocean, Fulton signed up for work and became a train dispatcher for the new line.

After the construction was completed, he became a land agent for the railroad, in charge of all the railroad's land between Colfax, California, and Ogden, Utah. He also founded the *Reno Evening Gazette*, a predecessor to today's *Reno Gazette-Journal*.

Giroux Street

Giroux Street is named in honor of Roland Giroux, a land developer who is best known for creating the "El Reno" style apartment in the 1930s. After Giroux's attempt to raise the rent was vetoed by the rent control board, the individual buildings were moved off the site and scattered about town. A few still remain.

Fun fact: In 1952, Roland Giroux donated some land to the city for a street on the condition that the city name the street after his friend John Kuenzli. Kuenzli later reciprocated, and wanted a street named after Roland Giroux. So, here it is. Now, to adapt the words of the late Paul Harvey, you "Giroux" the rest of the story.

See also Kuenzli Street.

Gould Street

Gould Street honors Warren Hill Gould, one of Reno's early livestock traders. He built the state's first creamery on the site of what is today Model Dairy. Gould not only almost single-handedly supplied the area's entire milk needs in the late 19th century, but he also quenched the milk thirst of San Francisco hotel guests.

Haskell Street

When Myron Lake deeded parts of the Reno town site to the Central Pacific Railroad, he did so on the condition that the railroad would put a station within the new town (then known as Lake's Crossing). Lake hired Dan Haskell to close the deal and make the terms official. Lake never rewarded Haskell with a street name. That came later with the development of this subdivision in 1907.

Prior to this deal, though, Haskell was co-operator of a store in Washoe City, at that time the county's largest settlement and county seat. He later became a state Assemblyman, representing Esmeralda County, and served one term in the first state Legislature, 1864–1866.

Hill Street

This short road just south of Downtown Reno commemorates Smith Hill, who founded the Reno Water Company in an effort to get fresh, healthy water to the fast-growing community.

Holcomb Avenue, Holcomb Ranch Lane

The only person to have two streets named after him in the Reno-Sparks area, Grove Robert Holcomb (1830-1905) arrived with his family in Gridley, California, in 1848 at the age of 18 to pursue the ranching business. When his father died, Holcomb lost all the cattle and all his money. He then walked three days to Virginia City looking for employment all along the way. Finding none, he then continued down the hill to Carson City, finally getting a job as a mill worker there.

During his time at the mill, he met his future wife, Sarah Lyell, who lived on a homestead with her father in the town of Huffaker's. They married in 1865, and in 1869 bought a 160-acre ranch near Huffaker's. This operation was successful, so they spent the next several decades expanding the ranch, buying more and more cattle and sheep.

Home Gardens Drive

This development was platted in 1939, at a time when home gardens were in vogue, given the depression and all; hence, the name. Rather like naming a street "Cabbage Patch Drive" in the 1980s, or "Pet Rock Pavilion" in the 1970s.

Hubbard Way

So named because it was once the main road into Hubbard Field, now known as Reno-Tahoe International Airport. The airport was named originally for Eddie Hubbard, the Boeing engineer who originally designed it. (Later, the airport was renamed for Senator Bruce Cannon, and finally *re*-renamed for a prominent local aquatic landmark, Lake Tahoe.)

Huffaker Lane

The name of this street is just about all that remains of the once-thriving settlement of Huffaker's, which was located at the site of what is now the Summit Sierra Mall.

Granville W. Huffaker (1831–1892) first settled in the area after driving hundreds of cattle to the Truckee Meadows from Salt Lake City in 1858.

The town had a population of over 300, with its own post office and V&T Railroad depot, making it by far the Meadows' largest settlement at the time. The town exported a lot of wood and produce to other locales within the Truckee Meadows.

Humboldt Street

This street is named after Humboldt County, Nevada, which, in turn, was named after the German explorer Friedrich Heinrich Alexander von Humboldt (1769–1859). Humboldt is best known for his exploration of Latin America and his work in the field of biogeography (the study of why species live where they do). Counties in Iowa and California are also named for him.

Hunter Lake Drive

Hunter Lake Drive is named in honor of the former lake, Hunter Lake, that once existed in the area now known as Caughlin Ranch. Hunter Lake, in turn, was named for John Hunter, an early settler to the Truckee Meadows. An associate of Hunter, John Stout, had built a bridge across the Truckee River five miles west of what is now Reno. During the flood of 1861, Stout drowned, and Hunter took over the operation of the bridge as well as the toll road. In the late 1890s, Hunter retired, selling the property to James Mayberry, who owned the mill in Verdi and wanted to expand his empire along the river.

Isbell Lane

So named because it passes along the edge of land once owned by the Isbell family. After moving to Reno in 1924, the Isbells ran a successful construction company for many decades before retiring in 1965. (Among their projects was the construction of Interstate 80 through Reno.) Their company's inventory was sold at auction in 1966.

Keystone Avenue

Named in honor of Keystone Canyon, which is a geologic feature of nearby Peavine Peak. There also was a small mining town on Peavine called Keystone, which at one point had a population of nearly 200.

Kirman Avenue

Richard Kirman was Governor of Nevada from 1935 to 1939. Born in Virginia City in 1877, he began his career in banking, eventually becoming a bank president. Before becoming Governor, he served in the State Assembly and on the University of Nevada Board of Regents. He was also the Mayor of Reno from 1907 to 1909.

During his time as Governor, the state advanced the "One Sound State" policy, which encouraged visitors to the state to become residents by emphasizing the benefits of living in its low-tax environment. Nevada advertised nationally that residents of Nevada had to contend with "no income tax, no inheritance tax, no sales tax, no tax on intangibles," and that the state had "a balanced budget and a surplus." (My, how times change, as today's Governor and Legislature try to figure out which corners to cut to keep the state's budget in the black.) When he finished his one and only term as governor, he went into ranching and hardware, dying in 1959.

Incidentally, Hoover Dam was completed during Kirman's time as governor.

Kleppe Lane

Kleppe Lane is named for John and Pearl Kleppe, who bought a ranch in this area in 1897. The couple's son, Ernest J. Kleppe (1902-1958), later served two stints in the State Assembly, 1930-1932, and 1940-1944. He then served on the Washoe County Board of Commissioners until his death in 1958.

A Quiet Wedding

John F. Kleppe of Glendale and Miss Pearl Motion of the Meadows Married.

The residence of Mr. And Mrs. C. C. Morton on the Virginia road was a scene of festivity Sunday evening, the occasion being the marriage of their daughter Miss Pearl to John F. Kleppe of Glendale. Only a few relatives and most intimate friends of the young couple were present. Mr. George Sauer acted as best man and Miss Ethel Peckham acted as bridesmaid. Judge Linn performed the ceremony.

At the conclusion of the marriage service and congratulations, the wedding party was invited to partake of a bountiful supper and full justice was done to the good things prepared.

The evening was pleasantly spent in music and conversation and at a late hour Mr. and Mrs. Kleppe left for their home at Glendale amid a shower of rice and old shoes.

Mr. Kleppe is one of our best known young farmers. He is popular with those best acquainted with him. Prosperous, energetic, and with a fair start in this world's goods, he will make a good home for the girl he has chosen as his helpmate.

Mrs. Kleppe is well known in the Meadows and is very popular. She also has many friends in Reno who will wish her unlimited happiness in her new sphere in life.

The happy couple were the recipients of a number of handsome wedding presents both useful and ornamental in establishing a new home.

The JOURNAL extends congratulations and hopes their best future will always be to them one long wedding day.

(*Nevada State Journal*, October 19, 1897.)

Kumle Lane

Kumle Lane was built as an access to the new Elks Lodge in 1960. The new lodge replaced the previous lodge which had been downtown, destroyed by a fire in 1957. The street is named after J.C. "Cliff" Kumle, longtime secretary of the Elks, who actually prevented that fire from becoming a major tragedy by sounding the alarm and evacuating the building quickly. (In the interim between the fire and the opening of the new lodge, the Elks met at the historic Mapes Hotel, now the site of City Plaza at First and Virginia.)

Kuenzli Street

This street runs on land donated to the city by Roland Giroux in 1952, on the condition that the city name the street after his friend John Kuenzli.

See also Giroux Street.

Lake Street

You may have noticed this street a couple of blocks east of the Reno Arch and wondered where the lake is. Having driven up and down this street, I can assure you that there is in fact no lake on Lake Street, so the beach ball and swim shorts won't be needed. So how did the street get its name?

There's No Lake on Lake Street!

Lake Street is in fact named for Myron Lake, the accidental founder of Reno. Wanting to find a way to profit from the mining boom in nearby Virginia City, Lake purchased an old washed-out bridge across the Truckee River from fellow settler Charles W. Fuller. The bridge was near the site of the modern City Plaza, just east of Virginia Street. Lake improved the bridge, then collected a toll of fifty cents for every horse, and one dollar for each carriage, that crossed the river. Knowing that the miners and other travelers would need a reason to cross the bridge, he also wisely plotted out the land on the north side of the river for the banks, bars, and other necessary businesses. This little town came to be called Lake's Crossing, then later, with the coming of the railroad, the town became known as Reno, after Civil War general Jesse Reno.

Reno, 1880

Reno is a smart little town, with a railroad passing through the center, with a large depot, and only one hotel at this time. The buildings are mostly one and two-story houses. Each building had a nice little yard and garden, for Reno is well watered by the Truckee River; therefore every person can raise his own garden. It is a very clean and, I believe, healthy town, with about five thousand inhabitants.* I believe the nearest mine is two miles off. There is also a coal mine somewhere near this town. The Hot Springs are about two miles off, where a large hotel and cure are erected. Here is where you can get your steam-baths every day in the week, which seems to cure the rheumatism like magic. You can see the steam from the springs full two miles off.

(From *Ten Years In Nevada, or Life on the Pacific
Coast*, by Mary McNair-Mathews, originally
published 1880 by Baker, Jones.)

The 1880 census for Reno showed an actual

population of 1,362 in the city; nonetheless, McNair-Mathews' quaint description of the area is worth noting.

Lancer Drive

This short street is so named because it gives access to McQueen High School, whose mascot is the Lancer, a renaissance cavalryman.

Lander Street

Named to honor Lander County, which, in turn, was named after General Fredrick W. Lander (1821-1862), who established a wagon route passing through the area en route from Wyoming to Oregon. Lander died in Virginia of pneumonia, after having served in the Civil War under the direction of General George B. McClellan.

Lemmon Drive

Named in honor of Fielding Lemmon (1824–1898) who ran a hotel on Peavine to accommodate the miners in the 1860s. He also tried to establish the town of Peavine City on the slope of the mountain. Following Lemmon's death, his family sold the land to Henry Anderson, and the area was known as Anderson Acres for decades afterward before once again becoming "Lemmon Valley." (Good thing there are no car dealerships in the area.)

Longley Lane

The name honors the Longley family, who were among the first settlers in the Truckee Meadows, establishing a ranch in the late 1860s.

Marsh Avenue

This street honors Washington J. Marsh, developer of the 1890s-era neighborhood that surrounds it, called "Marsh's Addition."

Marsh arrived in California in 1849—early in the Gold Rush—via the nautical Cape Horn route. Marsh began his mining career near Placerville, then moved to Plumas County to operate a cattle ranch.

By 1869, tired of California, the Marshes moved to Reno, building a mansion at the corner of Virginia and California Streets. Ten years later, the family sold the mansion to Myron Lake, the founder of Reno, for $5,000 and some cattle. The nomadic family moved south yet again, this time to Genoa, staying there until 1884, then traded that property for yet another one in Churchill County, west of modern-day Fallon. Finally, in 1887, weary of ranching, he sold that ranch, too, and retired to Los Angeles, California.

Marvel Way

This street had two names, neither official, until 1954. Then the city of Reno finally ended the confusion and named it after a longtime area dairyman. (It had been called by that name as well as Sunset Way for the previous several years.)

Matley Lane

Named for the Matley family, whose ranch once occupied the site of the current Reno-Tahoe International Airport.

Mayberry Drive

I had always assumed that the name of this country road was an allusion to the fictional yet idyllic town of Mayberry, made famous in the Andy Griffith Show. Actually, though, the road commemorates James Mayberry, who owned a mill in Verdi and provided much of the wood for the Capitol Building in Carson City.

McCarran Boulevard

It is appropriate that McCarran Boulevard loops around the entire Reno-Sparks area. Its namesake, Patrick A. McCarran, spent time all over the entire state, working in various offices for the people during his life, just as his namesake road winds up and down around the entire city, serving Reno and Sparks' entire population.

Born in Reno in 1876, Pat McCarran was first elected to the State Legislature in 1903, then went on to serve as District Attorney for Nye County from 1907 to 1909. He later served terms as the Nevada Chief Justice as well as sitting on the state Board of Parole Commissioners and the Board of Bar Examiners. In 1920, he represented actress Mary Pickford, nicknamed "America's Sweetheart" for her roles in such films as *Rebecca of Sunnybrook Farm* and *Taming of the Shrew*.

McCarran is best known for his work in the United States Senate, to which he was elected in 1932, serving there until his death in Hawthorne in 1954.

Mill Street

Mill Street nearly exactly retraces the route of the old country lane that once connected the mid-19th Century towns of Lake's Crossing and Glendale. Along the road, at the site of what is now the Grand Sierra Resort, was a sawmill owned by Charles H. Eastman. His mill processed logs that had been cut a few miles up the river at Crystal Peak, near Verdi.

Moana Lane

This main Reno thoroughfare is named after the nearby Moana Springs Resort, founded in 1905 by developer Charles T. Short. Short named his establishment after a similar resort he visited in Hawaii with that name. The resort changed owners several times over the years before the City of Reno bought the land in 1956. The city turned the resort into a public recreational center with ballpark and pool, in continuous operation until its closure in 2007. As of this writing, the city is making plans about the future of the pool and demolished former baseball stadium.

Though the natural springs no longer come to the surface, the water that once fed them is still under the surface and is used for heating of much of the nearby commercial and residential areas.

Reno drivers give thanks daily that Short did not visit the Kahalakaanapaliwailea Resort on that vacation.

RENO CAPITALISTS FIGHT FOR LAND

Reno, Nev., Nov. 19 – The efforts of capitalists to get control of the property lying south of Reno, and extending to Moana Springs, is growing into an open battle.

S. H. Waller, formerly superintendent of the Truckee River General Electric Company, headed by the Fleishhackers of San Francisco, has recently resigned his position with that firm and relinquished the management of the Nevada Transit Company, which operates a line from Sparks to the southern boundary of Reno. Senators Newlands and Nixon have recently acquired the ranches south of Reno and propose to operate a line over this property to Moana Springs. Interested with them and an equal stockholder is Herbert Fleischhacker.

Waller has, it is understood, declared war against the corporation and his engineers are surveying a road over this property just acquired by Newlands, Nixon, and Fleishhacker. It develops that Waller has a six-months option on the property so purchased by his rivals, giving the right of way over this property, and Waller declared that he will so build that the purchasers of over 400 acres of land will be deprived their right of way over it.

It was the intention of Newlands, Nixon, and Fleishhacker, principal owners of the property taken over by the Reno Development Company, to make a resort out of the place, establish an artificial lake and park and so improve the property that it would be attractive as a resort as well as a suburban residence section. If Waller, who is opposing them, succeeds in his plans, Moana Springs, lying at the southern extremity of the district, will maintain itself as a suburban resort of Reno, and the capitalists who have just spent $200,000 for about 400 acres will be reduced in their enterprise to selling suburban lots.

(From the *San Francisco Call*, November 20, 1906.)

Morrill Avenue

Enoch Morrill (1836–1920) did just about everything in his 84 years of life. Like many, he began his Nevada life as a miner, traveling west at the age of 27, settling in Aurora, then later in Washoe City. Wanting a break from mining, he then moved over to California, becoming a sheep rancher in Modoc County.

Three years later, wanderlust hit again, and Morrill returned to Nevada, buying a ranch several miles south of Reno. Then, in 1894, he sold that ranch, too, and bought one northeast of the city. Most of the land was subdivided into lots; the rest is now part of the UNR experimental farm, visible from I-80 near Wells Avenue.

Finally tired of ranching and country life altogether, he moved into the heart of downtown Reno. He died in 1920 at the age of 84.

Moya Boulevard

Keeping with aviation theme of many of Stead's streets, Moya Boulevard honors Moya Lear (1915–2001), who became chairwoman of the Lear Avia Corporation upon the death of her husband, Bill Lear, in 1978. A true philanthropist, she supported many organizations in the Reno area, particularly in the areas of arts, education, and, of course, aviation.

As an aside, Bill was an inventor in addition to being an aviator. His most famous inventions are the Learjet (of course), the autopilot, and the eight-track tape.

Newlands Lane

This residential street is named after Francis G. Newlands (1847–1917), who represented Nevada in the U.S. Congress from 1894 to 1902, and in the U.S. Senate from 1903 until his death in 1917. He is most famous for the Newlands Reclamation Act, which provided Federal money for irrigation projects throughout the west, including the Newlands Irrigation Project in nearby Churchill County. He also wrote the bill making Hawaii a U.S. territory.

As an early student of city planning, Newlands, along with some business partners, began buying up land in Washington D.C. with the intent to create a streetcar suburb. That area later became Chevy Chase, just inside Maryland at the District of Columbia border.

There is also a street in Fernley named after Newlands. That street is lined with warehouses, including that of amazon.com.

Nixon Avenue

This tiny street in the southwest area of Downtown Reno is named after George Stuart Nixon (1860-1912) a railroad telegraphy agent who later transferred to Nevada. He served in the state Assembly in 1896 and was elected to the U.S. Senate in 1905. But when he was serving the state's interests in Washington, his business in Nevada did not stop. Along with partner George Wingfield, he founded the Reno National Bank in 1906. The following year, to benefit from the mining boom in Esmeralda County, they opened a branch in then-lively Goldfield. In 1908, Nixon built the Winnemucca Opera House, then the largest theater in Nevada. The remains of Nixon's mansion, destroyed by a fire in 1979, are still visible from nearby California Avenue.

Patrick Avenue

This street honors Frank and Fannie Patrick, who owned a dairy farm in the area at the beginning of the 20th century. Fannie was known for her involvement in the 20th Century Club of Reno, a women's organization that was dedicated to philanthropy and making the Reno community a better place to live.

Peckham Lane

Named for George E. Peckham, who moved with his family to the Washoe County town of Galena from Massachusetts in 1864. He served in the State Assembly in 1901, and was a recognized expert in financial and banking matters despite his lack of formal education.

Plumb Lane

Named for the Plumb Family and Ranch, which was once in the foothills southwest of the Reno area.

Raggio Parkway

William Raggio (1926–2012) was the longest-serving State Senator in Nevada's history when he retired in 2011, having served there since 1972: that's 19 regular sessions, plus twelve special sessions. Before becoming a State Senator, he was in the Navy Reserve and United States Marine Corps Reserve. After discharge, he became the Assistant District Attorney and then District Attorney of Washoe County.

Ralston Street

This street on the edge of downtown Reno is named for William Ralston, a prominent Reno fixture during the city's early days. Along with his partners, William Sharon and D.O. Mills, he built the Virginia and Truckee Railroad, which connected Reno with the mining boom town of Virginia City 20 miles away. He also lent money to Leland Stanford to begin the construction of the Central Pacific Railroad, linking California with the rest of the country.

Ingeniously, Ralston arranged financing of the Virginia and Truckee Railroad so that while he and his partners got the profits of hauling the swag, the taxpayers of Washoe and Storey Counties got stuck paying for the cost of the railroad's operation.

Despite this ingenuity, Ralston was not responsible with his money. He often would lend money to anybody in need of it, without factoring in the person's ability to repay. (Sound familiar?) Eventually, the bank ran out of funds due to the bad loans, and the Board of Directors forced him to resign in August of 1875. He committed suicide in the San Francisco Bay that very day, but his name remains, a daily reminder to residents of the young city's up-and-down fortunes.

As an interesting aside, there is a city in central California to this day that was originally supposed to be named Ralston in his honor. Being a modest sort, he declined the city's offer, and the town became known as Modesto as a testament to his modesty. Today, that city of modest beginnings has a population of over 200,000 people and is a county seat.

See also Sharon Way in Reno and Mills Park in Carson City.

Redfield Parkway

Named in honor of LaVere Redfield (1901–1974), one of Washoe County's largest landowners. He moved to California during the depression, making a fortune by buying stocks other saw as worthless. Many of them eventually became very valuable.

As he became wealthy, he moved to Reno, slowly buying up as much land as possible while continuing to live a frugal lifestyle.

After his death in 1974, $400,000 worth of silver dollars—most in mint condition—were discovered in the basement of his ranch at Mt. Rose and Forest Streets. It's unknown why he kept them rather than putting them into a bank, but popular theories include his distrust of banks or his desire to hide his wealth from the Internal Revenue Service.

The Redfield Promenade shopping center, the Redfield Building at the University of Nevada, and the Redfield Campus of Truckee Meadows Community College are also named in his honor.

Ryland Street

Originally known as South Street. Renamed Ryland Street in honor of Richard Ryland (1835-1911), who came to San Francisco, like many others, looking for wealth. He did not find it in the gold fields, however, but rather in real estate, helping others buy and sell land and taking a commission on each purchase. In the 1870s, he was ready to leave San Francisco, so he moved east to Eureka, Nevada, got married, and moved to Reno to buy and sell real estate in that fast-growing town. He purchased land all over the outskirts of town, subdivided it, and sold it. He died suddenly of a heart attack in 1911.

> When Mr. Ryland moved to Reno the town had little to appeal to the settler. He was animated by several motives. He appreciated the benefits of the climate resulting from the altitude and dry air. He desired to be in convenient touch with the coast and to enjoy the alterations of the sea level and the mountain climate, for on the coast he had been much troubled by rheumatism. Chiefly, however, he realized that Reno would be the coming city of Nevada.
>
> On moving here, Mr. Ryland bought 34 acres, including the present site of his home on South Virginia street. Later he bought 27 acres more, sharing this ownership with Dr. Thoma and Judge

Cheney. Subsequently he acquired large tracts including a large tract on the southwest side which he subsequently sold. He acquired valuable downtown property in the business district, including the Ryland building, the Ryland and Levy block, the Lusich Annex hotel building on Second street, and other buildings on the west side of Virginia street of which he sold part interests to Judge Cheney and A. Manning.

Mr. Ryland was of a modest and unobtrusive disposition and sought few honors. His advice was invariably sought on business affairs and was given to the best of his knowledge, which was extensive. He was held in high respect as a man of strict integrity, in politics he was a democrat and took a lively interest in affairs. He did not seek public office, but served one term as county treasurer in Eureka county beginning in '77. At the time of the World's Columbian exposition in Chicago in 1892 he was appointed as alternate commissioner from Nevada with George Russell of Elko.

(From the Nevada State Journal,
November 12, 1911.)

Cheney and Thoma, by the way, also have streets named for them nearby.

Sadleir Way

Appropriately enough, considering its location at the main entrance to the Reno Rodeo grounds, Sadleir Way honors Charles Sadleir, former City Councilman and the first President of the Reno Rodeo. Prior to being elected to the city council, Sadlier was manager of the famous Riverside Hotel, originally founded by Myron Lake.

A little bit of trivia about this street: From the time the street was built in 1948 all the way until 2004, the name was officially but incorrectly spelled "Sadlier." To this day, both spellings are common.

Sharon Way

Named after William Sharon (1821–1885), a banker who, like many, came to the area and sought to make money from the gold and silver booms. He and his partner, William Ralston, lent money to the miners for operations, planning to profit from the mines upon the inevitable foreclosure.

After his partner's sudden death in 1875, Sharon took charge of Ralston's assets, including the Palace Hotel in San Francisco. He was elected to the U.S. Senate in 1875, serving one term before retiring to San Francisco.

See also Ralston Street.

Sierra Street

This street got its name because it originally connected to a road leading over the Henness Pass over the Sierra Nevada mountain range to the west of Reno. The name Sierra Nevada means "snowy mountain range" in Spanish, and is usually shortened to simply "Sierra" or "The Sierra."

Stead Boulevard

Stead Boulevard honors the former Stead Air Force Base, which operated from 1942 to 1966. Originally called Reno Army Airport, it was renamed Stead Air Force Base to honor the son of a local rancher, Croston Stead. Stead died in a mock dogfight in his P-51 Mustang in 1949.

In the mid- to late-1950s, the base served as the survival training ground for Army, Navy, Air Force, and Marine soldiers, as well as astronauts. The school at the base was broken into four categories: basic survival (prevention of drowning, hypothermia, etc.), combat survival, evasion and escape procedures, and counterinsurgency tactics.

Later, Croston's brother, William Stead, founded the nationally known Reno Air Races in 1964 to honor both Croston and the 100th anniversary of Nevada's statehood.

Steamboat Parkway

Steamboat Parkway is named for the nearby Steamboat Springs, which, in turn, got their name from the puffing sound each spring emits prior to eruption.

An early history of Nevada, published in 1881, briefly discusses the site's busy history up to that point: The springs were discovered in 1860 by Felix Monet and Mr. Cameron, who quickly sold the land to Dr. Joseph Ellis and Charles W. Cullins in 1861. Ellis built a hospital on site, along with a bathhouse to further the health of his patients. In 1861, Cullins sued Ellis for the rights to the property, a suit which dragged all the way until 1867, when the judge found in favor of Cullins. Cullins then burned down all of Ellis's improvements and started over, putting a railroad depot, hotel, and restaurant on the site. The V&T Railroad used the station for a year, and an entire town developed.

In 1873, Cullins, perhaps as some sort of divine retribution for burning down Ellis's original development, fell into one of the springs and died. In 1874, Mr. and Mrs. Rapp bought the property and improved it further.

Though the original buildings are long gone, the site remains as a place of refreshment for the area's residents and visitors to this day.

Mark Twain, on Steamboat Springs

I have overstepped my furlough a full week - but

then this is a pleasant place to pass one's time. These springs are ten miles from Virginia [City], six or seven from Washoe City and twenty from Carson [City]. They are natural - the devil boils the water, and the white steam puffs up out of crevices in the earth, along the summits of a series of low mounds extending in an irregular semi-circle for more than a mile. The water is impregnated with a dozen different minerals, each one of which smells viler than its fellow, and the sides of the springs are embellished with very pretty parti-colored incrustations deposited by the water. From one spring the boiling water is ejected a foot or more by the infernal force at work below, and in the vicinity of all of them one can hear a constant rumbling and surging, somewhat resembling the noises peculiar to a steamboat in motion - hence the name.

(Mark Twain, writing to the editors of the
Territorial Enterprise, the Virginia City newspaper
which made him famous, August 23, 1863.)

Stevenson Street

This street honors Charles Clark Stevenson (1826–1890), the first Nevada governor to die in office.

Before becoming Governor, Stevenson was a member of the Board of Regents of the University of Nevada. A strong supporter of the university, it was under his governorship that the university moved from Elko to Reno, to be closer to the majority of the state's population.

Sutro Street

Sutro Street commemorates Adolph Sutro's (1830–1898) contribution to the mining rush in nearby Storey County. Sutro, along with prominent local banker William Ralston, devised a method for removing water and gas from the mines of the Comstock Lode by drilling a tunnel through Mount Davidson. Upon completion, his tunnels daily drained three million gallons of water, and he quickly became known as the "King of the Comstock."

After making his fortune at the Comstock Lode, Sutro moved to San Francisco and personally paid for many public improvements to his new hometown: The best known of these are the Sutro Baths, destroyed by fire in 1966, and the Cliff House, which still stands today. The tallest structure in the city, a television antenna known as "The Sutro Tower," is also named after him.

Syler Court

In 2004, the western portion of the former Green Acres Drive was renamed Syler Court to honor William Syler, lifelong city resident, World War II veteran, and member of the Nevada National Guard.

Thompson Lane

Named for William Thompson, an associate of Christopher C. Powning. Powning had recently developed a subdivision west of Reno, and Thompson was interested in selling the health benefits of living in Reno. His idea was to develop a road to Incline Village at Lake Tahoe, as well as run a stage line along it to and from his Reno hotel. That road, built in 1891, is now known as the Mount Rose Highway, or Highway 431. Although paved and heavily traveled, it still—a century later—does not fulfill Thompson's wish to have an all-season road passable in any weather: it's frequently among the first roads to close or require chains during winter storms, and the last to reopen.

The road was the only efficient way from Reno to the North Shore until 1900, when a railroad branch line from Truckee to Tahoe opened along what is now California Highway 89, making access to the lake much easier.

Twin Lakes Drive

This is a very minor road, named Twin Lakes Drive because it runs between two small ponds.

Urban Street

This street is so named because it was once the northernmost street in the Interurban Heights subdivision, developed south of Reno in 1907. Later, the city expanded south, and this road became the southern city limit at one point. Today, of course, it is well within the city limits, which have expanded miles in each direction. A 1907 map of Interurban Heights shows the original development, which was demolished a decade later for the construction of the Reno Golf Club, which later became the Washoe County Golf Course.

Virginia Street

Virginia Street, Reno's main north-south artery, follows the route of the original road laid out by Myron Lake in 1865. Wanting his share of the fortune up in nearby Virginia City, Lake built a toll bridge across the Truckee River as well as a road leading to it. A century and a half after Lake built the road, it remains the main entry into Reno from the south. (It is also the main entry from the north.) Except now it's taxes, not tolls, that pay for its upkeep.

So, then, the question becomes: How did Virginia City get its name? Nobody quite knows for sure, but legend has it that the miner James Finney, upon accidentally dropping a bottle of whiskey on the ground, quickly christened the rapidly-growing settlement "Old Virginny Town," to honor his state of birth. The town soon became known as "Virginia City," and the rest is—quite literally, in this case—history.

Had Finney been born somewhere else, all those exit signs on I-580 might today read "Rhode Island Street," or the famous arch would today be spanning "Massachusetts Street."

Wedekind Road

This area was named for the Wedekind Mining District, located northeast of Reno near the current intersection of Pyramid Highway and McCarran Boulevard in what is now Sparks. Wedekind, a piano tuner from Germany, moved to San Francisco in 1851, and then on to Virginia City in 1861. He continued work as a piano tuner, but dabbled in mining and found it to be a much more lucrative industry.

In 1896, back in Reno, he happened across a lead deposit in the hills; upon investigation of the area, he then found silver, gold, and zinc, and the Wedekind Land Boom was on.

In 1901, Wedekind sold the mine to then-governor John Sparks, who invested more money into it for even more efficient extraction. Sparks, however, did not manage his money well, became bankrupt, and lost the mine to creditors shortly before dying in office in 1908. The mine remained in operation until 1961.

Reno's Mining Boom 1900

Reno, the up-to-date in everything, has now launched a gigantic mining boom, the likes of which has never before been witnessed.

We wish our neighbor all sorts of success in her new venture and trust that the bullion yield of Wedekind district will not fall short of that of the Comstock. We, of a mining turn of mind, delight in anything pertaining to mining. As in all other things, mining has its humor, but the fun furnished by the tenderfoot of the riverside burg has thus far surpassed any ever seen on a comic opera stage, for of course there is music to all of this, the tune of silver dollars.

They are now finding coin down there, so far

45

has nature assisted this lucky place, and it comes under the heading of "mining." A letter was received here to-day from a man who has found "indications" in the basement of a shoe store, asking if he could borrow a hoisting engine and a few mining cars. They will be sent over the grade to-night.

At 10 a.m. A dispatch was received from a professor of the University asking the different between a crosscut and a wheelbarrow. Dr ------ [line in original] asks of the Report whether silver is ever extracted from the ground in the form of spoons, and adds that he thinks he has a fortune in sight. As the mining editor is away we are forced to defer an answer to correspondents.

(*Nevada State Journal*, June 30, 1900.)

Wells Avenue

Wells Avenue is the primary road in the Wells Addition, platted in 1905 on the site of the former ranch of Sheldon O. Wells.

Wheeler Avenue

Many people likely think this street was named for Nevada's highest mountain, Wheeler Peak in White Pine County. But, it was not. Like many streets in Reno, this one is named for a prominent rancher. Samuel Wheeler (1868–1934) grew up in Stockton, California. He bought his first property in Washoe County at the age of 21 and went into the sheep ranching business with his brother and father. His herd grew to 5,000 head on 30,000 acres.

Wheeler married the daughter of some other ranchers, the Wells family. Upon his father-in-law's death, Wheeler subdivided the old Wells Ranch into the Wells Addition, naming one of the streets for himself.

Wilbur May Parkway

See Double Diamond Boulevard.

Yori Avenue (Central Reno)

This street honors the Yori family, who purchased a ranch on the Truckee River west of Reno. In 1884, the family developed its land into Lawton's Hot Springs, a resort featuring a casino with a restaurant and meeting hall, and an Olympic-sized pool. The resort closed in 1957, and later became the Holiday Lodge.

As an aside, the name of the original owner was actually Sumner Laughton; however, the first sign the Yori family ordered for the property misspelled Laughton's name. Rather than fixing the sign, they changed the name of the resort.

See also Yori Park.

Themed Streets In Reno

Given its location in a valley, it's no surprise that the area around Silver Lake and Reno-Stead airport would have so many streets named for mountains:

Alleghany Street

Andes Street

Cascade Street

Green Mountain Street

Ozark Street

Rocky Mountain Street

Teton Street

Ural Street

Many of the streets in Stead near Moya Blvd (named for an aviator, after all) continue that aviation theme. No surprise that The Names in Stead Fall Mainly On The Planes:

Beechcraft Drive

Corrigan Way

Corrigan Way deserves a bit of an explanation, since the story behind Douglas "Wrong Way" Corrigan (1907–1995) could fill a book of its own. And has, in fact. Corrigan, an accomplished aviator with his own Curtiss Robin plane, had long wanted to fly across the Atlantic ocean. He had logged numerous trips back and forth across the country, but still, the challenge of crossing the ocean awaited.

Flash forward to the summer of 1938. Having just arrived in New York after yet another cross-country flight, Corrigan wanted to continue his trip east to Europe. However, this was shortly after the disappearance of Amelia Earhart, so the authorities were not eager to grant transoceanic clearance. Officially, Corrigan decided to fly back to California instead, and filed a flight plan to that effect.

Corrigan took off from New York and headed east. His official intent was to fly east to avoid some buildings, then turn west and fly back to New York. However, due to a bad compass, cloud cover, and night, he never actually turned to the west: rather, he kept flying east. For hours, actually, until day broke, he noticed land, and soon discovered it was actually Ireland.

He landed in Dublin, nonchalantly told the officials he meant to land in California but got lost, and left it at that. We may never know whether or not he actually intended to cross the Atlantic that day and land in Ireland, but everyone bought his story, sticking him with the nickname "Wrong Way" Corrigan, a phrase that soon entered pop culture.

Cub Court

Piper Place

Red Baron Blvd

Sopwith Boulevard

Just "fore" fun, many streets adjacent to the former Northgate Golf Course in Northwest Reno have appropriate names:

Hogan Court

Maxfli Drive

Sand Wedge Lane

Spalding Court

Three Wood Lane

Titleist Court

The Kings Row neighborhood of northwest Reno has many royal names:

Commonwealth Circle

Crown Drive

Harold Drive

Jester Court

King Edward Drive

Majestic Drive

Prince Way

Royal Drive

Tudor Crest

Windsor Way

As somebody's joke, there is also a Cinderella Drive in this neighborhood, undoubtedly having some fun with the procession of princes.

The Galena area of south Reno has several streets named for cities in the west. Oregon cities represented are Corvallis, Medford, Bend, and Portland. Colorado gets Greeley and Fort Collins. The streets representing Montana are Bozeman, Great

Falls, and Missoula. Finally, for homesick Washington residents, there is Bellingham Drive, Kirkland Court, and Vancouver Court (or Vancouver Drive, take your pick).

In north Reno, an Atlas will tell you that the Greeks hold court: Socrates, Achilles, Isis, Diogenes, Demos.

MISCELLANEOUS FUN STREET NAMES IN RENO

I feel like I should go get some porridge and visit Mama Bear, Papa Bear, and Baby Bear courts in Cold Springs.

Somebody in the Northwest Reno area must have emigrated from San Francisco, for there you can find streets named Van Ness, Geary, O'Farrell, and Polk.

Climbing the Mt. Rose Highway, the road to a major ski resort, if you were to exit at Wedge Parkway you would enter a neighborhood with a series of streets named after famous ski re-sorts, such as Lake Placid Drive, Sugar Bowl Court, Telluride Court, and Whistler Ridge Drive.

Way out in east Reno near the Truckee River is an office park with a series of financial names, including, of course, Financial Boulevard. If that's not enough for you, try to put your Capital [Boulevard] into Wall Street, and then see if you have any Equity [Avenue] in it.

No surprise that NV Energy, the local power company, has office space in the area of Ampere Drive, Ohm Place, Joule Street, Reactor Way, and Energy Way.

Really geeky? Then try setting up a business on Technology Way, Sandhill Road, Trademark Drive, Innovation Drive, or Terabyte Court in south Reno. (Decades from now, terabytes will be as obsolete as slide rules. Wonder if they'll change the name?)

If you're wondering what Sandhill Road has to do with tech-nology, by the way, I will point out that Sand Hill Road in the

Silicon Valley is well known as the home of multiple venture-capitalist firms. A venture capitalist firm, or VC, is a business that specializes in funding startup businesses in return for a share of the new business's profit. Back in the go-go days of the late 90s, an approval from a VC firm was a cause of celebration among a "dot com" business. Of course, you also know what happened to most of those new "dot coms."

Plumb Lane, of course, has nothing to do with fruit, but near the Kietzke intersection, somebody had fun with the name and gave us Orange Lane and Apple Street. Yum!

Finally, if your invention doesn't pan out and you want to drive to an Ivy League college, there is always, in that same fruity area, Harvard Street (where the Costco is), along with Radcliffe, Duke, Lehigh, Auburn, Purdue, Clemson, and Vassar—that's a good start. Oddly, Dartmouth Drive is some distance away, further to the west near Shopper's Square Mall.

RENO PARKS

Pat Baker Park

Pat S. Baker was a graduate of the University of Nevada, Reno. During her tenure as the editor of the company newsletter of Sierra Pacific (now NV Energy), she often wrote columns supporting the development of a city park in the neighborhood. Eventually, because of her influence, the city agreed to the idea of a park, and it was built over a single weekend, opening on Sunday, July 19, 1968.

Barbara Bennett Park

This park is named for Barbara Bennett (1923–1993), who moved with her husband to Reno in 1964. She was best known for her crusade to end discrimination against women and her strong support of the Equal Rights Amendment. She was a co-founder of the

Nevada Women's Political Caucus, a group dedicated to ensuring that political candidates are aware of the needs and rights of women in the workplace. Because of her efforts, the voters of Reno and Washoe County began to support the idea of women as political candidates, and many were actually elected. Bennett herself was elected as the city's first female mayor, serving from 1979 to 1983.

John Champion Park

Named for naturalist John Champion (1945–1997), who loved the Truckee River and was a strong supporter of the natural environment. The Truckee River, he thought, was "a river people can see and touch and dangle their feet in. It must be a river you can ride your bike along, or fish in, or swim in. You've got to be able to float down its current or kayak through its whitewater, or simply stroll along, enjoying its beauty and wildlife." Champion called himself "The Truckee River Keeper," and took personal responsibility to keep the river a place people could do all those things.

Crystal Peak Park

This is actually a Washoe County Park, not operated by the City of Reno, and named for the once-thriving logging community of Crystal Peak, which encompassed this area in the 1860s. The community supplied the wood and other materials needed to build the Central Pacific Railroad, with the hopes that the railroad would go through and even stop at the town. No such luck: the railroad decided instead to stop in nearby Verdi, two miles south, and the town of Crystal Peak slowly faded into history. Verdi, however, grew, and later became famous as the site of the first train robbery in Nevada. Today, a state historical marker just off Front Street in downtown Verdi commemorates that robbery.

Crissie Caughlin Park

This park is on land donated to Washoe County in 1993 by its namesake's daughter, Betsy Caughlin Donnelly. Crissie Caughlin was a longtime rancher in the area, and was also influential in several women's organizations around the Truckee Meadows. Donnelly donated the land to ensure that her mother would get her wish: that the area around the river would never be developed.

See also Caughlin Parkway.

Mary Gojack Park

This park is named for Mary Gojack (1936–1985), who served one term in the State Assembly in 1972, and one term in the State Senate, serving there from 1974 to 1978. Her major legislative accomplishment was passage of the Parkland Bill, a law requiring that developers, not the city or county, pay for the creation of parks. She also lobbied against placing a sales tax on food and was a strong supporter of the Equal Rights Amendment.

Mary Gojack, on Equal Rights

"[The Equal Rights Amendment], most essentially, is a statesman's way of acknowledging what the realities of life in the United States are today. It is an acknowledgment that the breadwinners in 16 million American families, or one-fourth of our population, are females, not males. It acknowledges the heavy burdens of war are shared by all humankind. It acknowledges that we are willing to pass on to our daughters a heritage of equality—a heritage which heretofore has been reserved exclusively for our sons."

(Mary Gojack, speaking in support of the
Equal Rights Amendment, May 19, 1975.)

Highland Ditch Greenbelt

This area once held the Highland Ditch, first built in 1879. The ditch was a water delivery system designed by Alvaro Evans to compete with the already-established Reno Water Company. Evans used a series of pumps to move water from the river to tanks near the current site of Rancho San Rafael Park (on Washington Street), where it would be piped into the city. However, the ditch's main problem was that it would freeze each winter, and when it wasn't frozen, the water in the exposed ditch would get exposed to the elements and even the occasional dead livestock.

The ditch and its associated flume were in use for twenty years before Christopher Columbus Powning (developer of the Powning's Addition area of Reno) and others invested in major upgrades of the system and other competing water delivery companies. Portions of the ditch are still visible today, most notably at Evans Creek Trail, north of the university. However, the flume, which was once visible from I-80 and the railroad upon entering Nevada from California, collapsed in an earthquake in 2008.

Ducks, Dogs, and Water, 1880

Wild ducks seem to relish the seclusion that the reservoir grants. Quite a number have been shot there already this fall. Gunners are forbidden to send dogs into the reservoir. If a man shoots a duck and it falls into the water he must wait until the wind blows it ashore. If the winds don't rise, he must wait until the flies blow the bird to land. Under no circumstances must he send a dog in. If a dog falls in, the man mustn't go after him. If the man falls in, the dog mustn't go after him. The Water Company are determined to supply no cold man nor cold dog to their customers. They have agreed to furnish water, but not meat, and they will stick to their contract.

(Advertisement in the *Reno Evening Gazette*, October 5, 1880.)

Horseman's Park

This area was donated to the City of Reno by Cressie Caughlin, since Caughlin loved horses and wanted to ensure that people always had a place within the city to ride them.

Dorothy McAlinden Park

This park honors a longtime community activist for the Stead area, Dorothy McAlinden (1915–2003). She wanted to make sure that the area was not neglected by the city government, developers, or residents. Perhaps her best-remembered campaign was for the installation of sidewalks and street lights along nearby Stead Boulevard. Because of her love of the community, and her longtime service on the city's Neighborhood Advisory Boards, the city renamed Mayor's Park after her in 1994.

She also received the prestigious Distinguished Leadership Award from the American Planning Association, and the Nevada Library Association has named its annual award to classified employees in her honor.

McKinley Park

This park is named in honor of Former U.S. President William McKinley, who was President from 1897 to 1901. The McKinley Park School, which sits nearby, is one of the two remaining schools built at the turn of the century in a Spanish mission style. The school now serves at the city's Arts and Culture center. (The other remaining school, Mt. Rose Elementary off Arlington Avenue, still functions as an active public school.)

Pickett Park

This park, though commonly called "Hospital Park" because of Washoe County Hospital (now known as "Renown Medical Center") across the street, actually did not have an official name until 1947, when the city named in Pickett Park in honor of Samuel

M. Pickett, who served on the county Board of Commissioners from 1935 to 1945. Pickett's actions were instrumental in getting the county the title to the land the park is on. (Of course, it is now well within Reno city limits.)

Powning Park

Named in honor of Christopher C. Powning, who developed the first addition to the City of Reno, named, appropriately enough, "Powning's Addition."

Miguel Ribera Park

This park is named for Miguel Ribera, who was a well known restaurant owner in Reno for decades.

Ivan Sack Park

Named for Ivan Sack (1908–1985), who served his entire career with the U.S. Forest Service working to promote the wonders of nature to the public. He was well regarded as a botanical expert in the area, and loved living in Nevada.

Schiappacasse Park (pronounced "sheep-case")

The park is named for the ranching family that once owned the land where the park now sits.

Teglia's Paradise Park

Named for Roger Teglia, who bought the property in the 1950s and decided to turn the unused irrigation ditches and gravel pits into ponds. The city's $300,000 purchase, spread out over fifteen years, was controversial at the time. Even though he sold the property to the city in 1964, the ponds remain, a lasting memory of Teglia's efforts to beautify this otherwise run-down commercial area.

By the way, near the park, you may notice the "Charles Hendrickson Overpass" crossing over Oddie just west of Silverada. Many drivers assume that Charles Hendrickson was possibly a councilman or maybe somebody who got hit crossing this busy intersection. However, neither assumption is correct. Charles Hendrickson was a Reno Police Department traffic officer who took it upon himself to help kids from the nearby Cannan Elementary safely cross the busy intersection every afternoon. The overpass was actually prefabricated elsewhere and lifted into place at the intersection. The dedication ceremony, consisting of Hendrickson and children from Rita Cannan, was held February 9, 1970—meaning three generations of children have safely crossed Oddie.

Whitaker Park

Whitaker Park is named for Bishop Whitaker, who founded the Whitaker Seminary on this very spot in 1875. Whitaker noticed the need for a real institution for learning just for girls in the city, and pledged $15,000 in church funds to the project if the city would front the remaining cost. It did.

In 1876, Whitaker left the school (known locally as "Whitaker Academy") to return to Pennsylvania. Following its founder's departure, fewer and fewer students enrolled until the school finally closed in 1893. The building was used for several purposes before being torn down in the 1920s, including a hospital and asylum.

Wingfield Park

This park is on the site of a former amusement park on an island along the Truckee River in downtown Reno. The original owner of the lane, L.E.C. Hinkley, sold it to the Belle Isle Park Company, which developed an amusement park on the island in 1911. By 1915, however, its lender, the John S. Cook Company (of which George Wingfield was president) took over the land in a fore-closure sale. The company held the land for a couple of years, and then sold it in 1917 to the Reno Business Men's Association. In

1920, the association sold it to Wingfield, who then immediately sold it to the city for use as a park. In appreciation, the city named the new park after the man responsible for ensuring it would always remain a park.

In 1928, the park was damaged in a major flood, and Wingfield personally contributed funds to restore the park to its undamaged state.

To this day, Wingfield Park remains a popular recreational destination and hosts events almost every day in the summer and fall.

Wingfield made his money in mining and was a millionaire many times over while still in his twenties. Since he really had so much, he decided the best thing to do with it was to give it away. Wingfield was very generous with his money, later donating money for improvements to the First Methodist Church near Wingfield Park, a new hospital building for St. Mary's Hospital, and for a new summer camp at Lake Tahoe. He also donated land for a new school in a new subdivision. (That site was the original location of Billinghurst Middle School in Southwest Reno).

In 1912, Governor Tasker Oddie offered Wingfield the position of U.S. Senator, to replace his associate George Nixon, who had died in office. Wingfield, however, declined, knowing he could serve state better in private business. Despite his declining health, he continued in the mining business all the way until his death in December 1959.

Yori Park

Yori Park honors the Yori family, who established a ranch on the Truckee River west of Reno. In 1884, they opened Lawton's Hot Springs (named after their land's original owner), a resort featuring a casino with a restaurant and meeting hall, as well as a capacious pool. Pugilist Max Baer used the resort as a training facility before his matches in the 1930s.

See also Yori Avenue.

RENO SCHOOLS

Anderson

The original Anderson School, built in 1887, was built on South Virginia Street and named for William Anderson, an area rancher. The school was rebuilt at its current location in 1955.

Libby Booth

This may be the only misspelled school name in Washoe County. Nonetheless, it was named for Libbie C. Booth, born in Monterey, California in 1856. Since her parents died when she was young, she began teaching to make a living at the age of 15, in Hollister, California. (In fact, she was so young, many of her students were older than she was!) After marrying and moving to Reno in 1888, she continued her teaching career, teaching at the Central School, then the Southside School, and then becoming principal of the Whitaker School (site of today's Whitaker Park). She concluded her educational career by becoming principal of the new Orvis Ring School in 1910 before retiring in 1935.

She moved back to California in 1944 and died in San Jose in 1948.

Rita Cannan

Named for Rita Cannan, who became Principal of the Mary S. Doten School in 1931. Common belief is that Cannan was the first female school principal in Nevada, but later research has proven that to be incorrect: Hannah Clapp, of Capitol fence fame, was a principal as early as the 1860s.

See also Cannan Street.

Caughlin Ranch

Named for the former ranchland on which the school now sits. For more information, see Caughlin Parkway.

Archie Clayton

Like many schools in the Truckee Meadows, this one was named for a Washoe County School District member. The school opened in 1964 to relieve congestion at nearby Central Junior High.

Double Diamond

See Wilbur May Parkway, Double Diamond Boulevard.

Glenn Duncan

Named for a former Superintendent of Public Instruction, who had just died when this school opened in 1957.

Elmcrest

This school is named for the street it is on, Elmcrest Drive, likely so-named on the whims of a long-ago developer.

Galena High School

Named for the town of Galena, of which this land was once a part. As the name suggests (Galena is a type of lead ore once found in the nearby hills) the town was founded in 1860 for mining, but shortly thereafter turned its attention to a much more profitable business, lumber. In 1865, a fire destroyed the town, but a meager attempt was made to rebuild, and it survived on logging until 1880, when it disappeared to the history books. The mill in question was located at the site of the current Grand Sierra Resort, hence, Mill Street.

An Incident at Galena

Galena, like most mining and logging towns, had a lively, thriving atmosphere, as described by one of its residents, George E. Peckham. Note that I have added paragraph breaks, but otherwise, the wording is unchanged from Peckham's original account in Reminiscences of An Active Life, *his memoirs published in about 1920.*

A little incident happened at Galena some fifty five years ago when Jack Fraser, A. M. Lamb and myself were much more vigorous than now. I was the only one of the three that belonged to the Sons of Temperance of Galena, which will exonerate me from the charge of having taken part in the following incident and it is probable that A. M. Lamb and Jack Fraser were as innocent as I was.

A man by the name of Hollingsworth came to Galena in 1865 and engaged in business, keeping candy, nuts, pies and cakes for sale. He was a very temperate man and after he had been in business about four days and had not patronized any of the saloons in Galena a citizens' meeting was held in one of the saloons and a resolution was passed that no man would be allowed to remain in business at Galena more than three days unless he patronized the saloons. A collection was taken up to defray the cost of enforcing the resolution and several men offered their services free to furnish the necessary labor to make the resolution have the desired effect.

Two kegs of blasting powder were purchased, and a short time after midnight an excavation was made close to the front end of the building and the powder was placed in this excavation. Then a large mound of dirt and gravel was placed around and over the powder and about two o'clock in the morning there was a big explosion which woke me up. I was living a block or more from where the explosion took place and it seemed some little time after I woke up before gravel began to fall on the roof. The front end of the building where the explosion took place was badly damaged and many of the candy jars were broken but the proprietor, who was sleeping in the back room, was not injured. He took the hint, went out of business and left Galena the next day.

He afterwards went to work at the Eastman sawmill and was there in 1866 when I was working at the same mill. He felt pretty sore about the way he was treated at Galena until I explained to him the quality of the whiskey that was in use at Galena, describing, of course, how the barrels of whiskey were on tap while being hauled by teams from Sacramento over the mountains and how the teamsters afterward filled the barrels with water, and how this weakened whiskey had to be strengthened with powerful and peppery solutions after arriving at Galena and the peculiar effect it had on the people of Galena who had been used to drinking pure whiskey in California. After this showing of extenuating circumstances he said it looked very different to him and he would be careful after this not to judge them too harshly.

The "Eastman" Peckham mentions, by the way, supplied all the lumber that was needed to build the schoolhouse over in Glendale, free of charge, as his way of supporting the community.

Nancy Gomes

Nancy Gomes (1926–1979) was a former member of the Washoe

County School District. She also served one term in the Nevada State Assembly in 1976.

Huffaker Elementary

Named for the community of Huffaker's, once located near this spot. See Huffaker Lane.

Proctor R. Hug

Hug was born in 1902 in Elgin, Oregon, but moved to Tonopah, Nevada as a child. He was a star athlete at UNR, coaching and playing football, basketball, and track. After graduation, he coached at Sparks High School, and then became principal of that school. After that, he became superintendent of the Sparks School District, and then the assistant superintendent of the newly consolidated Washoe County School District.

After retiring from education, Hug served in the Nevada State Senate from 1966 to 1972. Hug died in 1991.

Echo Loder

Loder began teaching in 1890 at the old Sierra School, and later became principal of the original Mary S. Doten school in Sparks. In 1924, she moved to Northside Junior High, and stayed there until she retired in 1935. She died in 1953 at the age of 85.

Robert McQueen

Dr. Robert McQueen was an emeritus professor of psychology at nearby University of Nevada, Reno, at the time the school opened in 1981. Dr. McQueen was able to arrange the Washoe County School District's purchase of the high school site from the Bureau of Land Management for only one dollar.

Sarah Winnemucca

This school is named for Sarah Winnemucca, who—along with Pat McCarran—is one of two Nevadans honored in Statuary Hall in

Washington, D.C. Born a Paiute, in 1844, she dedicated her life to educating Paiute and Washo children as well as serving as a liaison for settlers to western Nevada.

She died in Montana in 1891.

SPARKS

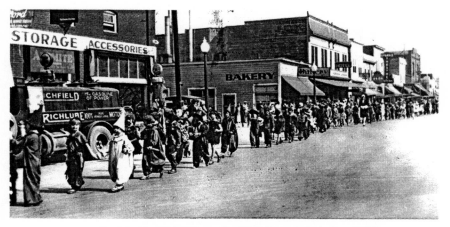

Jack's Carnival Parade, "B" Street, Sparks, 1930

From nothing, on the edge of the desert, to a thriving city of 3000 inhabitants is the remarkable achievement that Sparks, the division point on the Southern Pacific railroad, three miles east of Reno, has to boast of. Such a phenomena [sic] would be impossible anywhere else but in the west. Sparks is a railroad town, but that is not all. It is a thriving business place and its commercial interests, independent of railroad support, are growing rapidly. Small factories are starting up and Sparks is destined to expand its borders until they have become confused with Reno's outer rim.

Sparks was built over night. That is to say, was started in a night. What was Wadsworth one day, was Sparks the next. Wadsworth was transplanted on cars, houses were cut in two or shipped whole and placed on Sparks foundations. This happened because the Southern Pacific authorities concluded to make the latter place the division point on their main line across the continent.

While this action was the first cause, and the building so moved the nucleus of the city, they cannot account for the present size and growing importance of Sparks. That city is enlarging because of the enterprise of her citizens, and because of the many advantages of the place to the business man, to the professional man, and to the homemaker generally . . .

The climate, like that of Reno, is healthful, salubrious and invigorating. Sickness is rare and pestilence maladies unknown.

Much building is constantly going on, and labor receives remunerative and satisfactory compensation and there are no striking laborers nor other industrial disorders.

Altogether Sparks is a desirable place to live in and cannot be anything but prosperous and happy. It will continue to grow as long as people desire pleasant surroundings, a progressive community, healthful citizens, and sociable neighbors.

(Nevada State Journal, December 23, 1906.)

Baring Boulevard

Baring Boulevard honors Walter S. Baring, Jr. (1911–1975), who served Nevada in the House of Representatives from 1949 to 1953, and again from 1957 to 1973. Prior to that, he served in the Nevada State Legislature as well as the Reno city council.

Baring is perhaps best known for opposing the popular 3rd Street alignment of Interstate 80, wanting instead to route the new freeway well north of the central district along what is now McCarran Boulevard. Because of Baring's persistence, the final alignment runs a few blocks north of 3rd Street, close enough to be able to conveniently bring visitors to casinos' parking areas without entirely disrupting the central core.

Coney Island Drive / Galletti Way

Ralph Galletti was an immigrant from Italy who opened a tamale factory near this site in 1927. In 1945, he expanded into the brick building across the street still known as the "Coney Island Bar," in honor of the amusement park that stood across the street from the site. The park operated from 1909 to 1912. The last remains of the park were torn down in the 1960s for the construction of Interstate 80, but the name remains.

El Rancho Drive

This street name is all that remains of the El Rancho Number Two, an eighty-unit motel that opened near what is now the intersection of Prater Way and Victorian Avenue. The El Rancho Number Two was developed by Pete Cladianos, whose son later went on to develop the Sands casino along Arlington Avenue in downtown Reno.

Freeport Boulevard

This street name serves as a reminder of the state's Freeport Law, signed into law in 1949 by Governor Vail Pittman. It states that property stored in the state with the intent to resell is not subject to taxation, creating an entire warehousing industry. (Just as there are many warehouses around this neighborhood.) This idea was quickly copied: 27 other states quickly enacted similar laws, but not before Nevada, and the Truckee Meadows in particular, got a head start on the warehousing and shipping industry.

Galleron Way

Valentine Galleron was a Sparks City Councilman, murdered in 1987 in a most unusual fashion. Janine Hillman got two life sentences for hiring a couple to drop a television into his hot tub while he was in it, in an extortion attempt. Randy Howard and Valerie Fuentes pled guilty to the crime. Howard is still in prison serving two life terms without parole; Fuentes died of heart problems in 1994 at the young age of 32.

Originally, the death had been ruled accidental, but Galleron, despite his duress, was able to fool his extortionists by intentionally signing his name on the checks in a fashion other than his normal signature; this was how they were later discovered and indicted for the murder.

George Ferris Drive

This short road honors George Washington Gale Ferris, Jr. (1859-1896), most famous for inventing the Ferris Wheel in honor of the 1893 Columbian Exposition in Chicago. Born in Illinois, he moved to the Carson Valley at the age of two, then to Carson City a few years later.

Ferris attended college in California in 1876, then began his career as a civil engineer in Pittsburgh, Pennsylvania. Because of his well known talent for engineering, particularly with metal, the Columbian Exposition commissioned him to design the main landmark for the event. He eventually came up with the idea for the giant rotating wheel that is found at every county fair in the nation today.

Ferris's childhood home in Carson City (311 West Third Street) is today on the National Register of Historic Places.

Glendale Avenue

Long before there was a Reno or even a Lake's Crossing, John F.

Stone and Charles C. Gates were in charge of a ferry crossing of the Truckee River in present-day Sparks. Upon hearing of the plan for a new, more direct crossing of the river a few miles to the west, Stone and Gates improved their crossing by creating a bridge as well as developing a store carrying items useful to travelers. Call it a forerunner of the Seven-Eleven stores! By making an effort to maintain their road better than the proposed route, the pair planned to make theirs the main way across the river. In 1866, a couple built a hotel at the settlement, calling it the Glen Dale House. The name of the hotel later became the name of the new town site, later shortened to simply "Glendale." The town later succumbed to severe flooding but nonetheless lent its name to one of Sparks' major industrial streets.

Ice House Avenue

This road is named for the ice house that once stood at this spot. The Pacific Fruit Express (PFE) was a special train (owned by both the Southern Pacific and the Union Pacific) that would haul produce from California over the mountains, through the desert, and to the population centers of the Midwest and east. Unfortunately, though, without refrigeration, the fruit and vegetables would quickly spoil. Hence, during the winter months, the PFE would collect ice—which forms naturally in the Sierra, of course— and store it in huge warehouses along the route, one of which was in Sparks, just southeast of the current site of John Ascuaga's Nugget.

Kleppe Lane

The Kleppes first arrived in 1863 the area later to become Sparks. They operated a mule-team service between Virginia City, Nevada, and Truckee, California, and later turned to ranching.

Kresge Lane

Named for the S.S. Kresge Company, owner of Kresge and K-Mart stores. Its western distribution center was built on this street in the 1960s.

Lillard Drive

Honors James Lillard, who was mayor of Sparks from 1971 to 1979.

See also Lillard Park.

Nichols Boulevard

The original Mary Lee Nichols Elementary School, on Pyramid Highway and B Street, was named after a popular teacher at the nearby Sparks Grammar and High School. The school served students from 1912 to 1966. Now, nearby Nichols Boulevard stands in her honor.

O'Callaghan Drive

This street honors Donal Neil "Mike" O'Callaghan (1929-2004), who was Governor of Nevada from 1971 to 1979. As a Korean War veteran and former teacher in the Clark County city of Henderson, he had a special interest as governor in the welfare of the state's disadvantaged children and ensuring a steady supply of affordable housing in Nevada.

Oddie Boulevard

This major thoroughfare connecting the Reno Rodeo grounds to northeast Sparks is named after Tasker L. Oddie, who originally came to Nevada as manager of the Tonopah Mining Company in Nye County. He later served the state as Governor (1911–1915) and as U.S. Senator (1921–1933).

Pittman Drive

This street is named in honor of Vail M. Pittman (1883-1964), who served in the Nevada State Senate before he become the state's Lieutenant Governor.

Unlike many other Governors, who chose mining or ranching for their occupation, Pittman was a newspaper man. He had stints as manager/editor of several papers at various times, including the *Tonopah Miner*, the *Ely Daily Times*, and later the *Ely Record*.

He was elected as White Pine County's State Senator in 1924 and served one term. After his stint in the Legislature, he organized the White Pine Building and Loan Association. He was also President of several organizations in eastern Nevada, including the White Pine Chamber of Commerce, the Allied Counties Association, and Intermountain Development. The latter two groups were dedicated to promoting the region through creation of better roads to the area.

Pittman became Lieutenant Governor of Nevada in 1943, then became acting governor when Edward P. Carville resigned in 1945.

Pittman was then elected Governor outright in 1946, during a period of heavy growth in the southern part of the state. He lost his bid for reelection and left office in 1951.

Prater Way

Named for Nicholas C. Prater, an early rancher in the area. Prater granted land to the city of Sparks for another school (now Robert Mitchell Elementary). The street was originally known as "The County Road," until the city of Sparks renamed it in Prater's honor in the 1930s.

Probasco Street

George Anson Probasco was a developer of much of the area now known as Northeast Sparks, including the Greenbrae Shopping Center, one of the area's most prestigious addresses when it opened in 1958.

Pyramid Highway

So named because it is leads from Sparks to Pyramid Lake, thirty miles to the north. Pyramid Lake, in turn, was so named by explorer John C. Fremont, for its distinctive pyramid-shaped island.

John C. Fremont, on Pyramid Lake, 1844

Beyond, a defile between the mountains descended rapidly about 2,000 feet, and filling up all the lower space was a sheet of green water some twenty miles broad. It broke upon our eyes like the ocean. The neighboring peaks rose high above us, and we ascended one of them to obtain a better view. The waves were curling in the breeze, and their dark green color showed it to be a body of deep water. For a long time we sat enjoying the view, for we had become fatigued with mountains, and the free expanse of moving waves was very grateful. It was set like a gem in the mountains, which, from our position, seemed to inclose it almost entirely. Its position at first inclined us to believe it Mary's Lake, but the rugged mountains were some entirely discordant with descriptions of its low rushy shores and open country, that we concluded it some unknown body of water, which it afterward proved to be.

We encamped on the shore opposite a very remarkable rock in the lake, which had attracted our attention for many miles. It rose, according to our estimate, 600 feet above the water, and, from the point which we viewed it, presented a pretty exact outline of the great pyramid of Cheops. This striking feature suggested a name for the lake, and I called it Pyramid Lake; and though it may be deemed by some a fanciful resemblance, I can undertake to say that the future travelers will find much more striking resemblance between this rock and the pyramids of Egypt, than there is between them and the object from which they take their name.

(John C. Fremont, in his journal, January 10, 1844.)

Rice Street

Rice Street is named for A.T. Rice, an early dairy rancher in the Glen Dale community. His ranch was located near what is now the "Y" where 4th, Prater, and Victorian come together. Each day, he would sing and dance along his milk route, amusing his customers.

He was the prominent milkman in the area until 1891, when W.H. Gould set up his dairy at the site of what is now Model Dairy, west of Rice's former ranch. Because Gould was associated with Francis Newlands, it was Gould, not Rice, that eventually became the favored milk provider in the Truckee Meadows.

Russell Way

This street, like many others in the neighborhood, is named for a former Governor. In this case, it's Charles Hinton Russell (1903-1989), who governed the state from 1951 to 1958.

Charles Russell graduated from the University of Nevada in 1926, then became a teacher and, later, a miner. In 1929, he became editor of the *Ely Record*, then served in the State Assembly for three sessions (1935, 1937, and 1939) and the State Senate for two sessions (1943 and 1945). He then went on to became the state's Congressman, serving one term beginning in 1947. He was

73

elected governor in 1950, and re-elected in 1954.

During his term, the state saw a large increase in population, but the foresighted governor helped develop new agencies to handle the problems such an increase would create. For example, under his tenure, the Gaming Control Board came into being to regulate the casino industry.

After leaving office, he was the assistant to the president of the University of Nevada, in that position from 1963 to 1968.

Sullivan Lane

James O'Sullivan—at some early age he dropped the beginning of his family's name—came to New Jersey from his native Ireland in 1856. Four years later, he came through Panama to the West Coast, settling briefly in Sacramento, taking employment at a hardware store in that capital city. In 1862, he came to Nevada on a business trip and decided to stay. He bought an interest in the Glendale Hotel, only to sell it shortly thereafter after a heavy snowfall destroyed much of the building. Like many early settlers, he figured he might as well go into ranching, and ended up with a 240-acre plot.

Sparks Boulevard

Sparks Boulevard is named for the City of Sparks, which, in turn, is named for "Honest John" Sparks, who was Governor of Nevada when the Central Pacific Railroad founded the town in 1904. ("Sparks" was a better name for the town than "Harriman" and "East Reno," which were both briefly the name of the new settlement before the town's residents settled on naming it after the Governor.) Sparks was a rancher from Mississippi who made his way to Nevada via brief detours to Texas, Arkansas, and Wyoming, amassing his fortune all along the way. Finally arriving in Nevada in 1925, he built a new ranch a few miles south of the

Truckee River, which he called "Alamo Ranch" as a tribute to his Southern roots.

He was elected Governor of Nevada in 1902 and was elected to a second term, but died in office in 1908.

Victorian Avenue

Renamed from B Street in 1993, in an attempt to make downtown Sparks look like a turn-of-the-century railroad community.

Vista Boulevard

Named after the original stopping point of the railroad, Vista. Originally known as "Camp 37," the site had a truck stop, and later become a transportation hub with the addition of a landing strip in 1937 at the approximate site of what is now a Scheels sporting goods store. The Vista Airport became the home base of the Civil Air Patrol.

Numbered/Lettered streets in Sparks

Like many American cities, Sparks uses a numbered/lettered grid for its downtown streets, in which the streets running north and south are numbered, and those running west to east are lettered. In Sparks' case, 1st Street is the easternmost numbered street, and each successive street to the west has a higher number: 2nd, 3rd, 4th, etc. The southernmost lettered street is A, followed by Victorian (formerly B), C, D, and so forth.

But did you know that this was not the original arrangement of the town's streets as originally platted? In fact, the numbered streets ran east and west, and the ordinal arrangement started several blocks north of where the lettered streets begin in downtown Sparks today. Looking at the 1903 map of Sparks, here is the current name of the street, followed by its original name:

A Street / Nugget Avenue: Main Street west of current 15th

Street; Harriman Street east

B Street / Victorian Avenue: 2nd Avenue west of current 15th Street; Adams Street east

C Street: 3rd Avenue west of current 15th Street; Garfield Street east

D Street: Marsh

E Street: North 4th Avenue west of present-day Deer Park; Barclay St east of there

F Street: North 5th Avenue west of current 15th Street; Wright Street east (not to be confused with the never-renamed portion of Wright Street just south of current intersection of Prater Way and Pyramid Highway)

G Street: North 6th Avenue

H Street: North 7th Avenue

I Street: North 8th Avenue

4th Street: Hamilton Street

5th Street: McKinley Street

6th Street: Hayes Street

7th Street: Grant Street

8th Street: Lincoln Street

9th Street: Harrison Street

10th Street: Van Buren Street

11th Street: Jackson Street

12th Street: Monroe Street

13th Street: Madison Street

14th Street: Jefferson Street

Pyramid Highway/State Route 445: Lincoln St

16th Street: Elder Street

Rock Blvd: Deal Street

18th Street: Cedar Street

19th Street: Beech Street

20th Street: Ash Street

Themed Streets In Sparks

Transportation is a popular theme for streets in Sparks. Befitting a town nicknamed "The Rail City," an entire neighborhood of streets honors the iron horse:

Berkshire Drive

Caboose Court

Coachman Court

Conductor Court

Coupler Way (and Coupler Court)

Dutchman Drive

Engineer Court

Express Street

Golden Spike Drive

Jitney Drive

Junction Drive

Lionel Court

Locomotive Court

Pullman Drive

Railborne Drive

Stanford Way

Station Street

Aviation and meteorology themed street names fly high in Sparks, too:

Albatross Way

Contrail Street

Kittyhawk Drive

Lindbergh Lane

Rockwell Blvd

Sky Ranch Blvd

Soar Drive

Wing Way

Which dovetails (so to speak) to living things that fly:

Avian Drive

Eagle Nest Road

Eagle View Court

Eagle Wing Circle (somebody really likes eagles)

Gorget Court

Hawk Bay Court

Laughing Chukar Lane

Penguin Drive

Rockin Robin Drive (unfortunately, there is no Jay Bird Street anywhere in Sparks)

Silent Sparrow Drive

Sparrow Hawk Drive

Talon Court

Wild Hawk Drive

Since we're in the sky, don't get your head too far into the cloud-named streets, such as:

Billow Drive

Lenticular Drive

Mammatus Drive

Nimbus Court

Or stare starry-eyed at the constellation of astronomical names:

Arcturas Court

Axis Drive

Bellatrix Drive

Big Bang Drive

Big Dipper Court

Bootes Court

Borealis Court

Cassiopeia Court

Centaurus Drive

Cielo Circle (Spanish for sky. Also, interestingly enough, Spanish for heaven.)

Clearsky Road

Comet Court

Comet Linear Drive

Draco Drive

Early Dawn Drive

Eclipse Drive

Ganymede Court (Ganymede the largest moon of Jupiter, was, like many celestial objects, named for a mythological character, in this case, the prince of Troy.)

Gravity Street (I can really get down with this name!)

Hubble Drive

Kepler Drive

Lacerta Drive

Moon Vista Drive

Orion Drive

Perseus Drive

Scorpius Drive

Situla Court (Situla, Latin for "water jug," is a star in the constellation Aquarius.)

Solstice Drive

Star Vista Drive

Virgo Drive

Buon Giorno to the *vicinato* of Italian streets:

Bertini Court

Firenze Court

Panzano Court

Roman Drive

San Marino Drive

San Remo Drive

Sorrento Lane

Tivoli Lane

Tuscan Way

Venezia Drive

Certainly, don't "wine" about these names:

Bella Oaks Court

Carneros Drive

Cordoba Boulevard

Sienna Court (not to be confused with the Siena Casino in downtown Reno)

Silver Oak Lane

Stags Leap Circle

Appropriately, a set of streets right off Pyramid Highway plays homage to Egypt:

Aswan Street and Court

Dromedary Road

Egyptian Drive

Hyacinth Court

Pharaoh Court

Rosetta Stone Court

Sphinx Court

Suez Court

MISCELLANEOUS FUN STREET NAMES IN SPARKS

Somebody out there was popular with the girls, for in the area of Beau Court in Spanish Springs you'll find Alena Way, Tina Court, Veronica Court, Ember Court, Shelby Court, Carlene Court, Missy Drive, Nicole Drive, Sheena Drive, Kathy Terrace, Monica Court, Josefina Court, Catrina Court, and Megan Drive.

SPARKS PARKS

Aimone Park

This park is named after Earnest Aimone, co-owner of the Block S Store on B Street (now Victorian Avenue) in Sparks.

Melio Gaspari Water Park / Lazy 5 Regional Park

The Gaspari family, who owned a ranch just north of this area, came to the Spanish Springs Valley in 1917. The ranch, which eventually encompassed 7,000 acres, remained in the family until the mid 1990s. The park is named after Melio Gaspari as a tribute to his love of the area and its open space. Gaspari died in 2000, but his legacy lives on via the name of the park.

Les Hicks Jr. Park

The name of this park, built in 1994, honors Les Hicks Jr., who served as the city's Parks and Recreation Director.

Larry D. Johnson Community Center

Named in honor of a Sparks police officer killed in the line of duty in 1995.

Kestrel Park

Named for the American Kestrel, a small falcon that frequents the park.

Lillard Park

This park is named for James Lillard, who served as mayor of Sparks from 1971 to 1979.

See also Lillard Drive.

Longford Park

This park's name honors the town of Longford, Ireland, Sparks' sister city.

Pagni Ranch Park

Named for the former family ranch that once sat on this area. The city of Sparks bought the ranch in 1982, and used the land to build the park.

SPARKS SCHOOLS

Naming Rules

Washoe County School District Administrative Regulation 7551, adopted February 2003:

A. The Board of Trustees will select the names for new schools.

B. The Superintendent's office or his/her designee shall maintain a list of all names nominated or submitted for consideration for the naming of new schools. The list shall include:

1. Any geographical or geological name submitted

for consideration.

2. Any name of a resident of the community who has made a substantial or lasting contribution to education submitted by another person for consideration.

3. Any name of a person gaining state or national prominence submitted for consideration.

4. Submissions of nouns or adjectives representing positive values including, but not limited to, hope, courage, perseverance, etc.

Most of the schools in Sparks are named under the second possibility on the list. I have, however, elaborated on a few of the more interesting stories behind the names.

Bud Beasley

This school is named for Bud Beasley (1910-2004), an area athlete and educator. He was a star football player in Santa Cruz, California, and went to college at the University of Nevada. While there, he played football, baseball, and basketball. While attending college and playing sports, he was a student teacher at Mary S. Doten Elementary in Reno. Right after college, he moved out to Battle Mountain to teach school there, then returned to teach at Reno High School in 1936.

But his career as an athlete did not end after he became a teacher: Beasley also had a prolific career as a minor-league baseball player, playing for the Sacramento Solons and the Seattle Pilots.

He taught at Reno High until 1974, then continued by teaching physical education, history, and government at a variety of Washoe County schools up until 2003, only a year before his death.

George Dilworth

George Dilworth began his teaching career in a one-room school-house in Pennsylvania, but then later moved to Colorado to become the superintendent of schools in Gunnison. He also served as mayor of that city for one year. At various times, he was also the school superintendent in Rupert, Idaho, as well as in several Nevada school districts (Austin, Tonopah, and Virginia City) before becoming the Sparks superintendent in 1924. He retired from education in 1937.

Jesse Hall

This school is named after the first black teacher in Washoe County, hired in 1962. He later became the principal of Glenn Duncan elementary, and retired in 1992.

Lena Juniper

Named for Lena Juniper (1884–1965), an area educator. Originally from Ohio, she taught school there until moving with her husband to Reno in 1924. She taught at Robert Mitchell school in Sparks and McKinley Park school in Reno, teaching her last class in 1950.

Lincoln Park Elementary

So named because it sits on the site of what was once Lincoln Park, built as part of an early eastward expansion of Sparks.

Robert Mitchell

This school opened in 1904 in its original location as Sparks Grammar and High School, and Robert Mitchell was the first principal. In 1925, the school was renamed in his honor as a thank you for his years of service. In 1937, the original building was found to be unsafe and torn down, replaced by the current building next door to it in 1938. In the interim, the students attended various other schools throughout the Truckee Meadows.

Edward Reed

Edward C. Reed, Jr. was a longstanding member of the Washoe County School Board at the time of the school's opening in 1974. After Reed's long career as a tax attorney, President Jimmy Carter appointed him to the federal court in 1979, Reed served as the chief judge for the district from 1986 to 1992. He died June 1, 2013, at age 88.

Miguel Sepulveda

This school, the first in Washoe County named after a Hispanic, is named for the founder of *Ahora!* ("Now"), a newspaper for Hispanics. Also, Sepulveda founded the Hispanic Chamber of Commerce, and co-founded Nevada Hispanic Services.

Yvonne Shaw

Yvonne Shaw was born in Idaho in 1937, and died in Nevada in 1999. She taught at several area schools, including Sparks Junior High, Hug High School, and Reed High School. But her interest was not just with the kids: she also taught adult education for Washoe County and served on the Nevada State Board of Education.

CARSON CITY

Nevada State Capitol Building, 1875

One of the most famous former residents of Nevada's capital, Mark Twain, had something to say about the town he lived in for a short time. In *Roughing It*, he writes about his first view of the city after a twenty-day journey:

> At noon we would reach Carson City, the capital of Nevada Territory. We were not glad, but sorry. It had been a fine pleasure trip; we had fed fat on wonders every day; we were now well accustomed to stage life, and very fond of it; so the idea of coming to a stand-still and settling down to a humdrum existence in a village was not agreeable, but on the

contrary depressing. Visibly our new home was a desert, walled in by barren, snow-clad mountains. There was not a tree in sight. There was no vegetation but the endless sage-brush and greasewood. All nature was gray with it. We were plowing through great deeps of powdery alkali dust that rose in thick clouds and floated across the plain like smoke from a burning house. We were coated with it like millers; so were the coach, the mules, the mail-bags, the driver—we and the sage-brush and the other scenery were all one monotonous color. Long trains of freight wagons in the distance enveloped in ascending masses of dust suggested pictures of prairies on fire. These teams and their masters were the only life we saw. Otherwise we moved in the midst of solitude, silence and desolation. Every twenty steps we passed the skeleton of some dead beast of burthen, with its dust-coated skin stretched tightly over its empty ribs. Frequently a solemn raven sat upon the skull or the hips and contemplated the passing coach with meditative serenity. By and by Carson City was pointed out to us. It nestled in the edge of a great plain and was a sufficient number of miles away to look like an assemblage of mere white spots in the shadow of a grim range of mountains overlooking it, whose summits seemed lifted clear out of companionship and consciousness of earthly things. We arrived, disembarked, and the stage went on. It was a "wooden" town; its population two thousand souls. The main street consisted of four or five blocks of little white frame stores which were too high to sit down on, but not too high for various other purposes; in fact, hardly high enough. They were packed close together, side by side, as if room were scarce in that mighty plain. The sidewalk was of boards that were more or less loose and inclined to rattle when walked upon. In the middle of the town, opposite the stores, was the "plaza" which is native to all towns beyond the Rocky Mountains—a large, unfenced, level vacancy, with a liberty pole in it, and very useful as a place for public auctions, horse trades, and mass meetings, and likewise for teamsters to camp in. Two other sides of the plaza were faced by stores, offices and stables. The rest of Carson City was pretty scattering . . . There were sights to be seen which were not wholly uninteresting to new comers; for the vast dust cloud was thickly freckled with things strange to the upper air—things living and dead, that flitted hither and thither, going and coming, appearing and disappearing among the rolling billows of dust— hats, chickens and parasols sailing in the remote heavens; blankets, tin signs, sage-brush and shingles a shade lower; door-mats and buffalo robes lower still; shovels and coal scuttles on the next grade; glass doors, cats and little children on the next; disrupted lumber yards, light buggies and wheelbarrows on the next; and down only thirty or forty feet above ground was a scurrying storm of emigrating roofs and vacant lots.

It was something to see that much. I could have seen more, if I could have kept the dust out of my eyes. But seriously a Washoe wind is by no means a trifling matter. It blows flimsy houses down, lifts shingle roofs occasionally, rolls up tin ones like sheet music, now and then blows a stage coach over and spills the passengers; and tradition says the reason there are so many bald people there, is, that the wind blows the hair off their heads while they are looking skyward after their hats. Carson streets seldom look inactive on Summer afternoons, because there are so many citizens skipping around their escaping hats, like chambermaids trying to head off a spider.

Carson City is still similar in a lot of ways, even as the town itself has grown in the intervening 150 years. (The almost-daily closure to trucks of portions of the 580 freeway through Washoe Valley is a gentle reminder of the power of the "Washoe Zephyr" Twain humorously wrote about.) True to its roots, Carson still resembles a down-home suburb more than a capital city, with the Capitol and various state buildings thrown in almost as an afterthought among the shopping centers, residential develop-ments, office complexes, and big-box stores lining the freeways. Carson City seems like any other American town, but its unique Wild-West history is portrayed in its street names.

Carson Street

The main street through the capital is named after frontiersman Christopher "Kit" Carson (1809-1868), who headed west at an early age to trap and hunt in the areas now known as Colorado and New Mexico. Reputation well established, he traveled with John C. Fremont on a mapping expedition with the Army Corps of Engineers in the 1840s. He later became an agent for the Ute and Apache tribes in New Mexico, and even led a group of volunteers during the Civil War.

Carson Valley, a few miles to the south of downtown Carson City, is also named for Kit Carson.

Washoe, 1860

I was rather agreeably surprised at the civilized

aspect of Carson City. It is really quite a pretty and thrifty little town. Situated within a mile of the foot-hills, within reach of the main timber region of the country, and well watered by streams from the mountains, it is rather imposing on first acquaintance; but the climate is abominable, and not to be endured. I know of none so bad except that of Virginia City, which is infinitely worse. The population was about twelve or fifteen hundred at the time of my visit. There was great speculation in town lots, going on, a rumor having come from Salt Lake that the seat of government of Utah was about to be removed to Carson. Hotels and stores were in progress of erection all about the Plaza, but especially drinking and gambling saloons, it being an article of faith among the embryo sovereigns of Utah that no government can be judiciously administered without plenty of whisky, and superior accommodations for "bucking at monte." I am not sure but there is a similar feature in the California Constitution; at least, the practice is carried on to some extent at Sacramento during the sittings of the Legislature. Measures of the most vital importance are first introduced in rum cocktails, then steeped in whisky, after which they become engrossed in gin for a third reading. Before the final vote the opponents adjourn to a game of poker or sledge, and upon the amount of Champagne furnished on the occasion by the respective parties interested in the bill depends its passage or defeat. It was said that Champagne carried one of the great senatorial elections; but this has been denied, and it would be dangerous to insist upon it.

91

(From J. Ross Browne, "A Peep at Washoe,"
Harper's Magazine, December 1860.)

Corbett Street

Corbett Street honors the Corbett brothers, Daniel and William, carpenters who arrived in Carson City in 1860 to profit from the rapid development of the Comstock Lode. They built several hotels in the town to cater to the town's new residents and visitors. In 1868, William Corbett was elected to the Nevada State Assembly, where he served one term.

Curry Street

Curry Street is named for Abraham Curry (1815-1873), the man generally regarded as "the father of Carson City." He and his partners, John Musser, Benjamin Green, and Frank Proctor, purchased 1,000 acres in what was then known as Eagle Valley and laid out the town. In a rare moment of foresight, Curry reserved 10 acres in the center of town for the erection of a Capitol building, should the town be chosen as territorial capital. Which, of course, it quickly became, after fending off competition from nearby Virginia City.

Curry also built the Nevada State Prison, the Carson City Mint (now the state museum), and the Virginia and Truckee railroad shops in Carson City.

After establishing the city, Curry was elected to the Territory Assembly in 1862, then the Territory Senate in 1863. He died in 1873.

As an aside, Eagle Valley was named for the Eagle Ranch, so named because the proprietor, Frank Hall, happened to shoot an eagle on his property in 1851 and hang it over the door. Yet another example of a trivial and ordinarily forgotten incident of everyday life becoming the basis for a geographical name in

Nevada.

See also Musser Street, Proctor Street.

Elizabeth Street

This street is among several in the city's historic area named for the Phillips Family, who platted one of the first additions to the capital. Elizabeth Street honors Elizabeth Phillips, the family matriarch, who lived in Carson City from 1859 to 1870.

See also Phillips Street.

Long Street

This short street is named for John F. Long, who was hired by Abraham Curry to survey the proposed town site of Carson City, in Eagle Valley. Long advised Curry that the area would not be hospitable and suggested he try forming the town somewhere else. Curry refused.

After the survey, Curry was not able to pay Long's fee and offered him a piece of land in the new city. This time, it was Long's turn to refuse: he would rather be owed money than owe a seemingly worthless, inhospitable parcel. Long did, however, accept the position as the town's first Postmaster when the post office was established in the new town in 1858.

Planning for Carson City, 1876

When [Long] examined the premises he doubted very much the propriety and feasibility of the enterprise, and urged its abandonment. Curry had not forgotten his pledge to the speculators of Mormontown, to build a city of his own, and no argument could deter him from his seemingly rash enterprise, and in the face of natural objection, and notwithstanding all the reasonings urged by the less sanguine, who looked upon the plan as a foolish one, the survey of the site progressed to completion, and for the first time Carson City, that being the name given it, figured as a city on paper only. The streets were made wide for the reason that by pursuing that plan the plot would be larger, which, of course, would give it more prominence.

(*Nevada Tribune*, July 22, 1876.)

Lyon Lane

Named for adjacent Lyon County, which, in turn, was named for Nathaniel Lyon (1818-1861), the first Union General to die in the Civil War, at the Battle of Wilson's Creek.

General Lyon was a popular guy, apparently: he has three other counties named for him, in Minnesota, Iowa, and Kansas.

Musser Street

This street is named for Col. John J. Musser, one of the men who first laid out the town of Carson City. Musser, along with his partners Abe Curry, Benjamin Green, and Frank Proctor, purchased the land then known as "Eagle Ranch"—now downtown Carson City—from John Mankins in 1858. Mankins, regrettably, is not among the early residents of Eagle Valley honored with a street name, but Mankins Park in northern Carson City is named for him.

See also Curry Street, Proctor Street, John Mankins Park.

Nye Street

This street honors James W. Nye (1815–1876). Nye had a well established law career in New York, serving as District Attorney, then judge, then president of the New York City Metropolitan Board of Police, before being appointed by President Abraham Lincoln as Nevada's first territorial governor in 1861. In 1864, immediately after statehood, Nye was elected as one of Nevada's two delegates to the United States Senate, where he served two terms before losing his bid for a third term.

Nevada's largest county, Nye County, is also named for him.

Ormsby Boulevard

This street is named after Major William Ormsby, one of the first residents of the Eagle Valley. When Abe Curry was selling the original plats in the new town of Carson City, Major Ormsby was among the first to buy. In fact, he bought the plat immediately west of the central plaza, with the intent of building a hotel on the site.

After getting his hotel up and running, the major then led an army of volunteers to fend off Indian attacks on the new settlement. In 1860, his army attacked a group of Paiutes at Pyramid Lake, 100 miles north of the valley. Disorganization and poor planning led to a crumbling defeat of Ormsby's army, and only about 25 of the men returned to the valley. Ormsby was among those killed in the battle.

Major Ormsby, however, was remembered several years later when the new State of Nevada named its counties. The State named the area surrounding Carson City "Ormsby County." The area kept that name for a century until 1969, when the Legislature consolidated the county with the municipal government of Carson City.

A little trivia: Because of this consolidation, Carson City is the only area west of the Mississippi River that is not part of any county, though Carson City is generally considered to be a county for state matters such as voting, car registration, etc.

Phillips Street

Phillips Street honors Henry and Elizabeth Phillips, who platted one of the first additions to the capital city in 1862 and built a home in the newly developed area. In 1867, five years after creating the new addition on the west side of the town, Governor Henry G. Blasdel was about to foreclose on a loan against the couple's house. The couple settled out of court and moved to

Sacramento. However, the street they named after themselves remains to this day.

On a historic note, the name of this street had been misspelled as "Philips" on street signs for decades until 1997, when the *Reno Gazette-Journal* discovered the error based on old records. The embarrassed city quickly corrected the gaffe. (Carson City is not alone in misspelling street names: the city of Reno had its own mistake. See Reno's Sadlier Way.)

See also Elizabeth Street.

Proctor Street

Proctor Street, of course, is named after Frank Proctor (1828–1892), who, like most early Nevadans, moved west as part of the 1849 gold rush. After serving two terms as the assessor of Sierra County, California, the nomadic Proctor moved to Ione City, Nevada. As a prominent citizen, he served as Nye County's delegate to the 1864 state Constitutional Convention, as well as a State Senator during that Legislature's first three sessions, in 1865, 1867, and 1869.

Following his stint in the Senate, he moved to Elko briefly, then returned to Carson City, this time to serve as a clerk in the Assembly, for the 1871 session. He then began traveling around the country, getting a chance to help form the government of yet another state in 1884, participating as a delegate in Montana's Constitutional Convention. He died in 1892, completing a life of faithful service to fellow citizens all over the west.

See also Curry Street, Musser Street.

Roop Street

Roop Street honors Isaac Roop (1822–1869), one of Nevada's earliest settlers and its first territorial governor. After arriving in Nevada with his family in 1851, he moved to the Honey Lake area north of Reno, which at the time was thought to be part of Lake

County, Nevada. There, he founded Rooptown, later renamed Susanville in honor of his daughter, and Lake County, named for the prominent lakes in the area including Honey Lake and Pyramid Lake. However, an 1864 survey found that Susanville was actually part of California, and the area formerly thought to be in Nevada became Lassen County, California, while the part of Roop County that actually was in Nevada became part of Washoe County.

Though Roop was now actually a Californian, he continued to live in the town he founded, serving as the Lassen County District Attorney until his death in 1869. His daughter Susan lived until 1921 in the town named for her.

Saliman Road

Saliman Road is named for a former music director at Carson High School, Al Saliman (1921–1967). His most noted accomplishment was marching with the school in the Rose Parade in 1964, the only time the school has been in that prestigious event.

Stewart Street

This major north-south street is named for William M. Stewart (1827-1909), one of the early residents of Carson City. Stewart came west to California to try his fortune in the gold rush. After making a small fortune, he became District Attorney for Nevada County, then Attorney General of the State of California in 1854.

In 1860, because of his now well established legal career and knowledge of the mining industry, he moved to Virginia City to serve the legal interests of the prospectors there. After statehood, Stewart helped write the state's original Constitution. He was elected as one of the new state's first U.S. Senators in 1864, then reelected twice, serving a total of three terms in the Senate.

Stewart's most famous act as a United States Senator was writing the Fifteenth Amendment to the Constitution, which provides that the right to vote "shall not be denied or abridged by the United States or by any State on account of race, color, or previous condition of servitude." Nevada, not surprisingly, was the first state to ratify the new amendment.

After the Comstock mining boom, the state's economy began to stagnate. To remedy that, Stewart proposed in Congress that Nevada annex part of southern Idaho Territory, to take advantage of the growing economy in that area. Because of the new territory, he also suggested that the state capital move to Winnemucca, a more central location in the newly expanded state. President Grover Cleveland opposed the move, however, and the proposal disappeared entirely once Idaho became a state in its own right in 1890.

Senator Stewart Reminisces

At the time the [first Territorial Legislature of 1861] was about to convene there was a sharp contrast between Carson and Virginia City for the location of the capital. My family resided at Carson, but I had practiced more often at Virginia City. Previous to the bringing in of water from the Sierra Nevada Mountains, Virginia City was very unhealthy on account of the bad water; consequently I made Carson my place of residence. There was a lively contest in Carson for the member of the council, corresponding to the State Senator in the organized states.

A committee inquired of me the morning before the election where I thought the capital out to be, and I told them by all means at Carson, where the climate was excellent, the water good, which would make it a permanent town; whereas Virginia City was a mining town and not a suitable place for the capital. They did not disclose the purpose of asking me this question. I remained in Virginia City until after the election, and when the votes were counted I had more than two-thirds of them. There was nothing for me to do but serve.

Knowing that I had been elected for the purpose of locating the capital at Carson, I remained at home during the time the members of the Legislature were coming in from different parts of the Territory. I inquired of each how he wanted his county bounded and where he wanted the county-seat. Each one told me, and a framed a bill dividing the Territory into counties and making Carson the capital.

Virginia City lacked a few votes of half the Legislature. A large delegation came down, confident that they would locate the capital at Virginia City. All the counties were arranged to suit the members outside of Virginia City, and it was understood that any change in the programme would be disastrous to them in arranging the county boundaries. The Virginia delegation debated the question in a very enthusiastic manner, but we on the outside kept quiet until the vote was reached, when our programme was carried by three votes, the number that we anticipated.

I am sorry that I was forced to make so grave a mistake in arranging the programme, but I was compelled to take the course I did in order to make Carson the capital. The four counties of Ormsby, Storey, Lyons [sic], and Douglas are so near together that a horse and buggy can be driven to each of the four county-seats in half a day, and the expense of carrying on so many county governments is a great burden upon the people and upon the

State. It is hoped that the time may come when the people themselves will arrange the counties and the county boundaries in spite of the official cliques that live about the court-houses.

(From *Reminiscences of Senator William M. Stewart of Nevada*, George Rothwell Brown, ed., 1908.)

Wright Way

This street, best known as the home of the state Department of Motor Vehicles office, is named for state engineer W. Otis Wright.

Themed Streets in Carson City

As befits the state's capital, several streets are named after other western states, including Colorado, California, Idaho, and Utah.

A few streets in the southern part of the city honor formerly thriving mining towns in Nevada, such as Tuscarora, Goshute, Pioche, and Baker.

Since the railroad plays such a big role in Carson City's history (as it does in much of the rest of Western Nevada, as well), there are a few train-themed streets just south of downtown: Trolley, Pullman, Caboose, and, of course, Railroad.

Remembering the native population of Nevada is easy with street names like Washoe, Paiute, Shoshone, and Oneida. (The Shawnee and Cherokee, two tribes not found in Nevada, are not found in Carson City, either, but have streets named for them just beyond the city limits in unincorporated Douglas County.)

Near the airport, Carson City has its fair share of scientific streets, too: Watt are you doing Salking Fermi, because there's also Kelvin, and he was a real Joule. Pretty Hytech stuff. (I haven't even mentioned Newton, Faraday, or Tesla yet.) Since there is an airport nearby, it's only fair to have Lockheed, Boeing, and Convair Drives there as well. Nice to see I did my Research.

CARSON CITY PARKS

Fuji Park

This park sits on part of the land formerly occupied by the Ormsby County Poor Farm. Established in the 1860s, this was the place that the less fortunate members of the community could go to live and work. Residents would work on the farm in exchange for $10 a month and dorm lodging. This farm actually survived all the way until 1965, when the last four residents of the farm moved to nearby nursing homes.

That year, the city received a gift of $20,000 by Basil Woon, an author who had retired in the community, asking that the money be used to establish a park named for his wife, Fuji.

Ross Gold Park

Ross Gold was the city's first parks director. Hence, a park is named for him.

John Mankins Park

John Mankins, one of the most colorful characters in early Nevada/Utah Territory history, once lived in a cabin not far from the site of this present-day park. Many of the original settlers of the Eagle Valley (the valley in which Carson City sits today) had to quickly abandon their claims and return to Utah, per the instructions of leader Brigham Young. Mankins, sensing a way to quickly profit, bought up their properties with the intent of selling later. He called the area Mankins Ranch, enjoyed it for a few years, and in 1858 parceled it off and sold it to Abe Curry, John Musser, and Frank Proctor. You can read about them elsewhere in the book, but they are regarded as "the fathers of Carson City" for first laying out the plan of the future capital.

Mankins left the area once again, but his descendants still live in Carson City to this day.

Mills Park

Named for Darius Ogden Mills (1825–1910). He is best known in Carson City for being the owner of the Virginia and Truckee Railroad, the only link between the Comstock and the Central Pacific Railroad. He also was the owner of the Bank of California, which he rescued from the brink of insolvency after William Ralston's shenanigans (see Ralston Street, Reno, for more info.)

John D. Winters Centennial Park

This park sits on the land that once belonged to John D. Winters (1909–2007), a lifelong Nevada rancher and dairy operator who gave a lot of money, time, and land to Carson City and its schools. He had a special interest in water and conservation. Other public facilities that used to be on his land include Carson Middle School and Eagle Valley West Golf Course.

Winters' other community involvement included the Rotary Club, serving on the boards of Carson-Tahoe Hospital and Western Nevada College, helping create the 1960 re-enactment of the Pony Express, and chairing the Native Nevadan Committee for the state's centennial in 1964 (hence, the park's name).

Ronald D. Wilson Memorial Park

Ronald D. Wilson, who died in 1997, was the city's purchasing director, and was instrumental in getting the bonds to improve the city's parks back in the 1980s. The $3.75 million bond paid for the Centennial Park softball fields, the pool at Mills Park, and the soccer fields at Edmonds Sports Complex.

CARSON CITY SCHOOLS

Al Seeliger

Named for a former superintendent of Carson City schools. Prior to coming to Carson City in 1953, he had taught in Mina, Panaca, and Fallon.

Empire

Named for the community of Empire City, which stood near here in the 1860s and 1870s.

Originally a ranch owned by Nicholas Ambrosia, the locale was known as "Dutch Nick's." In 1860, Eugene Angel laid out a town, the site of the first mill on the Carson River. Lumber cut from Tahoe would be sent downriver to Empire City, then put about the railroad to Virginia City for use at the mines.

Empire City once had a population of 700, a dance hall, several saloons, and a schoolhouse hosting about 40 children.

Ultimately, it was a natural event that led to Empire's downfall: On March 16, 1907, a heavy snow turned to heavy rain. By the time the storm finally ended on March 20, it had destroyed several bridges across the Carson River and a dam, and had submerged at least half the homes in the community. The community was never rebuilt.

A Surveyor's View, 1881

Three and a half miles north of Eagle Ranch, now Carson City, the overland emigrant and stage road struck the bank of the Carson River, and there Nicholas Ambrosia located a ranch and kept a station, his claim being recorded March 24, 1855. The station became known as 'Dutch Nick's.' which name it bore long after the locality had been surveyed into lots and streets, and was officially known as Empire City. The town site was laid out in March, 1860, by Eugene Angel and other surveyors, and the name it now bears given it.

The fine water-power here afforded by the river, and its convenient access to the mines of the

Comstock Ledge, were the inducements for making a town. Several large quartz mills were built, as has been mentioned in the history of Ormsby County [now dissolved], and the town has always been busy and prosperous. Within the town are the Mexican and Morgan Mills, and others in the vicinity. Two miles below is the Brunswick Mill which, when in operation, employs 200 men.

At Empire is the depot of the wood business of the Carson River, the many thousand cords of firewood, mining timber and other classes of lumber floated down that stream are here caught in booms, landed and transferred to the cars of the Virginia and Truckee Railroad which passes through the place, and bourne to their destination. Fifty thousand cords of wood were thus brought to market in 1880.

Among the places of business are four saloons and one large store. The present population is 150.

(From Thompson and West's *History of Nevada With Illustrations and Biographical Sketches of Its Prominent Men and Pioneers*, 1881.)

John C. Fremont

Named for one of the first explorers of the area, John C. Fremont (1813-1890), sometimes known as "The Great Pathfinder." Upon leaving the military and leading four explorations of the new American west, he moved to California and became one of that state's first two senators. He is also believed to be one of the first whites to see Pyramid Lake north of Reno, as described elsewhere.

Fremont, being an explorer, has a legacy in many, many, places, with several states naming a city and/or a county after him: California, Colorado, Idaho, Iowa, Michigan, Nebraska, New

Hampshire, Ohio, Utah, Wisconsin, and Wyoming. And that's not even mentioning Fremont Street, the major street in downtown Las Vegas, nor Fremont Peak in northern California, Fremont Island or the Fremont River in Utah, or even the Fremont Bridge over the Willamette River in Portland, Oregon.

Eagle Valley Middle

Named for the valley in which Carson City sits. Carson City does not, as is commonly believed, sit in Carson Valley; rather, Carson Valley is the next valley south. (Think Minden and Gardnerville.)

See also Curry Street.

SOUTH SHORE LAKE TAHOE

Emerald Bay, 1910

This beautiful lake was originally named Bigler, after a distinguished politician, who held the position of Governor of California—John Bigler. It was so named by a gentleman who had a high admiration for the name of Bigler. The beauty of the scenery, the crystal clearness of the water, the inspiring purity of the atmosphere filled the soul of Bigler's friend with poetry, and he called this lovely spot Bigler. It was just a tribute to the popularity of the Governor among his friends; but no governor on earth can enjoy every man's friendship. Bigler had enemies like other governors—some because they wanted office and couldn't get it; others because they wanted a contract and couldn't get it; and many because they wanted to be governor themselves.

When this distinguished gentleman ceased to be Governor of California he was made a minister to South America. It was then discovered by both friends and enemies that the name was inappropriate and lacked euphony; friends had nothing more to hope; enemies nothing more to fear. Who the deuce is John Bigler, said they, that the finest lake in California should be called after him? Let us blot his ugly name off the map and call this beautiful sheet of water Lake Latham or Lake Downey. But here commenced a squabble between the friends of these eminent gentlemen relative to their respective claims. Latham, it was true, had served with honor in the Custom-house—had held the Gubernatorial chair for a few weeks, and subsequently had become United States Senator. But then Downey had vetoed the Bulkhead bill.

Pending this difficulty, a hint from some obscure source came very near resulting in the selection of a name that would doubtless have afforded general satisfaction, since it could be claimed by a great many people throughout the state—the name of Brown. It was brief, pointed, and popular: Lake Brown! But what Brown? There were thirty-six Browns in the Penitentiary, besides several more who ought to be there; and at least forty-four Browns were candidates for the Legislature or inmates of the Lunatic Asylum; so that it was difficult to see what Brown would be specifically benefited by the compliment. The name itself scarcely presented sufficient claims over all other names to be selected merely on account of its euphony. So Brown was dropped; and between Latham and Downey it was impossible to come to an equitable decision. The name of Bigler remained unmolested for several years longer.

In due time, when both Latham and Downey were both thrown overboard, the discussion of the question was renewed—every prominent man in the

State claiming that the lake should be named after himself. Finally, as popular sentiment could not fix upon the name of any white man, it gradually settled down in favor of the supposed Indian name—Tahoe—which was the first word spoken to the discoverer by a solitary digger, whom he encountered upon its shores. "Tahoe!" cried the digger; and it was at once assumed that "Tahoe" meant "Big Water"; but I am assured by an old settler that "Tahoe" means "Strong Water"—in other words, "Whisky"—so that this magnificent lake, formerly called Bigler, is now literally "Lake Whisky!"

(From J. Ross Browne, "Washoe Revisited,"
Harper's Magazine, May 1865, pp. 692-693.)

Al Tahoe Boulevard

This street commemorates Almerin Sprague, who developed a hotel in 1907 near the site of present day Al Tahoe Boulevard And US-50 and named it the Al Tahoe Resort, after himself. A small community, and even a post office, grew up around the area.

Frank Globin bought the hotel in 1924, and it remained in business, expanding all the while, until 1968 when it closed for good. His name lives on in the Globin Building, a block down US-50 to the north.

Bigler Avenue

Bigler was the lake's original name. See the introduction to this section above.

Emerald Bay Road

Emerald Bay is so named because its colors are much greener than the rest of the lake, due to its fairly shallow depth.

The first settlement in the era was in 1863, when Ben Holliday built a summer home in the area. Dr. Kirby bought more land around the bay in 1884 to develop a resort. That land changed hands several times before ending up in the hands of Mrs. Lara Knight, who built Vikingsholm Castle and built a small "teahouse" on Fannette Island, the lake's only natural island.

Knight died in 1945, and Lawrence Holland, a Nevada rancher, bought the property, only to resell it to Harvey West. In 1953, West sold the property to the State of California for one-half its assessed value, and it has remained state property ever since.

Incendiarism – The Offender Caught.

CARSON (Nev.), May 20th. - By the stage driver of Benton's line from Glenbrook, we learn that the Emerald Bay House was to-day destroyed by fire at the hands of an incendiary. It seems that the scoundrel who had set the fire had taken possession of the premises while Jack was visiting Dr. Kirby in Virginia. Jack caught the villain and tied him to a tree while he went for help. No further particulars.

(*Sacramento Daily Record-Union*, May 21, 1879.)

DISAPPEARANCE OF A LAKESIDE MAN

Hotel-Keeper Matthews Is Missing From His Home.

RUMORS OF A FLIGHT.

Creditors Fear That His Going Means Money Lost to Themselves.

HE TOOK HIS ASSETS ALONG.

He Was the Lessee of the Emerald Bay Resort on the Shore of Tahoe.

LAKESIDE, Lake Tahoe, Cal., Aug. 30.—C. W. Matthews, who leased the Emerald Bay resort, is missing and it is hinted that he has with him the entire earnings of the season and will not come back. The account books in connection with his hotel have been mutilated and pages extracted so that his debts and assets cannot be correctly estimated. On the evening that he left he informed the owner of the place, to whom he is still indebted for the lease, that he was going to Truckee on business and would return in the morning. He took with him over $1500 in checks in addition to about $1000 in coin and greenbacks. On arriving at Truckee he boarded a west-bound train, and has not been heard from since.

Matthews' sister, wife and mother departed a few days before, and it is intimated that they took all of his property, as none remained at the bay. Captain Lees of San Francisco will be notified to hold Matthews for breach of contract.

Among his creditors are several prominent San Francisco firms and firms in the vicinity of Tahoe, including the Truckee Lumber Company, the Co-operative Fruit Company and Fand, Bliss & Co.

(*San Francisco Call*, August 31, 1896.)

Friday Avenue

This street is so called because it intersects US-50 at the site of what was once Friday's Station, a Pony Express stop where riders switched horses. The station was operated by Martin "Friday" Burke and James Small, and was an important stop as it was one of the last places to rest before climbing mountains, no matter which direction the rider was going.

The station long outlasted the Pony Express: the Park family purchased the site in 1896 and continued to use it as a hotel, butcher shop, restaurant, and meeting hall up until the 1990s. There also was a blacksmith shop, which still stands on the site of the Edgewood Golf Course: the rest of the former grazing land is now buried under the towering casinos and parking garages of the Casino Row.

See also Park Avenue.

Hank Monk Avenue

See entry below.

Horace Greeley Avenue

James Henry "Hank" Monk was the driver of a stagecoach line between Virginia City and Sacramento from the 1850s all the way until his death in 1883. Monk became famous nationally after giving a nerve-wracking ride to journalist Horace Greeley. It is that ride in which Monk gave his most memorable quip: "Keep your seat, Horace. I'll get you there on time!" The story is perhaps best told by this poem, written by Joaquin Miller and published in the *Sacramento Daily Record-Union* on December 24, 1887:

> The old stage-drivers of the brave old days!
> The old stage-drivers with their dash and trust!
> These old stage-drivers they have gone their ways,
> But their deeds live on, through their bones and dust;
> And many and many a tale is retold
> Of these daring old men in the days of gold:

> Of honest old Monk and his Tally-Ho,
> When he took good Horace in his stage to climb
> The High Sierras with their peaks of snow,
> And 'cross to Nevada, "and come in on time;"
> But the canyon below was so deep—oh! So deep—
> And the summit above was so steep—oh! so steep!

> The horses were foaming. The summit ahead
> Was as steep as the stars on a still, clear night,
> And steeper and steeper the narrow route led,
> Till up to the peaks of perpetual white;

But the faithful old Monk, with his face to the snow,
Sat silent and stern on his Tally Ho;

Sat silent and still, sat faithful and true
To the great, good man in his charge that day;
Sat vowing the man and the mail should "go through
On time" though he busted both trace and stay;
Sat silently vowing, in face of the snow,
He'd come in on time with his Tally-Ho!

But the way was so steep and so slow—oh! so slow!
'Twas silver below, and the bright silver peaks
Were silver above, in their beauty and snow!
Where eagles swooped by with their bright, shiny beaks;
When sudden out-popping a head snowy white—
"Mr. Monk, I must lecture in Nevada to-night!"
With just one thought that the mail must go through;
With just one word to the great, good man—
But weary—so weary—the stage wheels drew
As only the weary old stage wheels can—
When again shot the head; it came shrieking outright:
"Mr. Monk, I MUST lecture in Nevada tonight!"

Just then came the summit! And the wide world below.
It was Hank Monk's world. But he no word spake.
He pushed back his hat to a high peak of snow!
He threw out his foot to the great strong brake!
He threw out his silk! He threw out his reins!
And the great wheels reeled as if reeling snow skeins!

The eagles were lost in their crags up above!
The horses flew swift as the swift light of morn!
The mail must go through with its message of love,
The miners were waiting his bright bugle horn.
The *man* must go through! And Monk made a vow,
As he never had failed, why, he wouldn't fail now!

How his stage spun the peak like a far spider's web!
It was spider and fly in the heavens up there!
And the swift swirling wheels made the blood flow and
    ebb;
For 'twas death in the breadth of a wheel or a hair.

113

Once more popped the head, and the piping voice cried:
"Mr. Monk! Mr. Monk!" But no Monk replied!

Then the great stage it swung, as if swung from the sky;
Then it dipped like a ship in the deep jaws of death;
Then the good man he gasped, as men gasping for
    breath,
When they deem it is coming their season to die.
And again came the head, like a battering ram,
And the face it was red, and the words they were hot:
"Mr. Monk! Mr. Monk! I don't care a ——
Whether I lecture in Nevada or not!"

— Joaquin Miller

When President Rutherford B. Hayes visited Nevada in 1880, he specifically requested that Monk be his stagecoach driver.

Lyons Avenue

Named for Rev. Patrick Lyons, first pastor of St. Theresa Parish, established in 1951. Lyons died in 1958 at the young age of 38, and the street was renamed for him later that year.

Kingsbury Grade

This road, originally called the Georgetown Trail, was built as a toll road in the early 1850s. In 1854, C. D, Daggett bought 640 acres at the bottom of the road, and the road was renamed for him—Daggett Pass.

Then, in 1860, two surveyors, McDonald and Kingsbury, improved the road more, shortening the journey between Sacramento and Virginia City. Though the tolls are long gone, the name lives on.

SACRAMENTO AND WAGON ROADS.

While we cheerfully concede to the citizens of other cities, towns and counties a commendable degree of enterprise in furnishing means to build wagon roads over the Sierra Nevada, we feel justified in claiming that the people of Sacramento city and county lead the column as wagon road builders. They began early and they continued the good work. They interested themselves early in the efforts making to open a road by way of Placerville through Johnson's Pass. The necessity for such a road was urged by this paper in season and out of season, long before the precious metals were known to exist in such quantities east of the mountains. Sacramentans were active in 1856 in their advocacy of the passage of the Act appropriating $100,000 to open a wagon road from Placerville to Genoa, through the pass known as Johnson's. Five thousand dollars were added to defray the expense of a survey. The Courts decided the Act unconstitutional, but its passage secured the survey of the route, which, though, was mainly accomplished by the liberality and enterprise of the citizens of Placerville. The failure to obtain State aid delayed, but did not defeat the object. In 1858 a considerable work was performed on the route by means of money collected by subscription in Placerville and Sacramento. The $2,800 raised in this city was expended in grading a road down the first summit into Lake Valley. Previous to the completion of that grade it was almost impossible to cross wagons by that route.

An enterprising stage company had run a line of stages over for several months, but a stranger would have declared, upon taking a first view of the trail, that to get a stage coach up or down it was impossible. It was, however, accomplished daily for some time before the grade was completed; after that was finished, though far from being what the one into Lake Valley now is, the great difficulty on the route was considered as overcome. It answered the purposes for which it was needed during the days of the Pony Express, the first month of the Overland Mail, and withstood the wear and tear of the first two years of the silver excitement in Washoe.

But the enterprise of Sacramento was not satisfied with what had been done, and in 1858, with the co-operation of El Dorado [County], succeeded in getting a special Act passed which authorized the people of each county to tax themselves to the amount of $25,000, the money to be expended in building a bridge over the American river, and in opening a road from that point to the Summit. The money was collected and expended, and a pretty good mountain road opened from Brockliss' Bridge [about a mile west of Bridal Veil Falls on modern US-50] to Strawberry. The early building of this road undoubtedly excited a large influence in concentrating the travel to and from Nevada Territory on that route— though the grade then made has been to a considerable extent abandoned for a rival road, which is located on the opposite side of the river. The efforts of the city and county of Sacramento ended with the expenditure of the $25,000; from that time forward the work of creating wagon roads was taken up by individual citizens; and to-day a large portion of the private roads between Placerville and Genoa are owned by Sacramentans.

They were built by Sacramento capital. In 1860 Kingsbury & McDonald surveyed and made a beginning on the celebrated graded road through

Daggett's Pass, on the Eastern Summit, and opened it to the public in 1861. In the Fall of that year they began work on their grade into Lake Valley, which they completed in 1862, and at the same time opened a good road through the valley. We do not know the amount of capital invested, but it must have been largely over $50,000. While the latter work was progressing, another Sacramento company was employed in building what is known as the Ogilsby grade [Oglesby Grade, on the opposite side of the river from modern US-50 between Whitehall and Silverfork], on the south side of the American river, commencing at the Junction House and uniting with the old road again a few miles below Strawberry. This enterprise was consummated by the aid of a still larger amount of Sacramento capital. With the exception of the sections built by Swan & Co., the toll roads between the Junction House and Genoa are mostly owned by citizens of Sacramento.

Last Winter some of our citizens obtained a charter from the Legislature, and they are now engaged in building a road from the head of Lake Valley to Silver Mountain and Aurora. But this does not end the chapter. Something over a year ago a company was organized in Sacramento to build a wagon road on the Dutch Flat route across the Sierra Nevada [later, this became US-40, now the modern I-80]. The estimated cost was $100,000, and stock to that amount was mainly subscribed by some of our business men and capitalists. A beginning was made last Winter, but the real work was not entered upon until last Spring, and from the time the season would admit the company has had employed on the work from one hundred and fifty to three hundred men. From Dutch Flat to the Summit—a distance of about forty miles—the road is completed, or will be by the 6th of November. It is, as we are informed by those who have traveled it, a superior mountain road. The grade at no point exceeds ten inches to the rod*, while the width will admit of the passage of teams at any place along the line.

From the Summit east into the Truckee valley—a distance of seven miles, and some of it very heavy work—the contractors have until Spring to complete the job; but we learn from one of them that they now have six of the seven miles finished, and with six weeks of good weather could complete the work. They have found it a difficult matter to obtain laborers; they have paid as high as forty-five dollars a month, and could not then obtain all they wanted, and had to resort to Chinese labor. They are now employing a hundred and fifty Chinamen, and a hundred white men. The same wages have been paid by the company on this side of the Summit, and then it was found difficult to obtain the desired number. From the foot of the grade in the valley of the Truckee the company will open a road down that valley to the Henness Pass road, a distance of fourteen miles. This will be done in the Spring, at an estimated cost of $10,000. The cost of the road, when fully opened, will exceed the estimate of $100,000. After glancing at the statement of the number of roads in which our citizens have invested their money, we think the reader will agree with us that Sacramento is entitled to the credit of taking the lead in wagon road enterprises.

(*Sacramento Daily Union*, October 30, 1863.
Paragraph breaks added for clarity.)

*A rod is a unit of measure equal to 16 feet, 6 inches. Therefore, the described ascent is equivalent to a 5% grade on today's roadways. [That is, $100*(10/(16.5*12)) = 0.0505$. This is the only math in this book, I promise.]

Park Avenue

Honors the Park family, which owned various businesses in the area in the early part of the 20th Century.

See also Friday Avenue.

Spooner Summit

Named for Spooner's Station, a stopping ground along Johnson's Cutoff (as the current US-50 was then known) in 1863. The small waypoint had a hotel and blacksmith shop so travelers could rest and re-provision for the taxing journey ahead.

In the mid-19th century, Spooner's Station was a logging area. Logging trains ran regularly from Glenbrook (several miles north) to Spooner's, then put onto a flume for transfer to the V&T Railroad for use for construction in Carson City and the Comstock.

The modern road over Spooner was first built in 1913 as part of the Lincoln Highway and was slowly modernized over the ensuing decades, finally being widened to its current four-lane configuration in the 1950s.

Tallac Avenue

Named for Mt. Tallac. "Tallac" is a Washoe word meaning "Great Mountain."

Themed Streets in South Lake Tahoe

There are a few neighborhoods with themed names within the city of South Lake Tahoe.

Given that South Lake Tahoe abuts Nevada and is the first part of California many people see, it's appropriate that there is a collection of streets named after that state's major cities in the middle of town: Merced, San Jose, Alameda, Pasadena, Oakland, Riverside, Fresno, Berkeley, San Francisco, Modesto, Tulare, and Los Angeles. (Oddly, Stockton and Lodi Avenues are several blocks away and don't even intersect any of the "city" streets.)

Quite a few streets in the southwest part of town are named after women. Among them are Shirley, Anita, Hazel, Patricia, Eloise, Glorine, Barbara, Rose, Edna, Becca, Janet, Anne, Norma, Jean, Marjorie, Alma, Bertha, Dedi, Julie, Melba, and Margaret. This appears to be a quite common theme among street names in general, however. (Guys, we have a few, as well: Charles, William, Martin, Bruce, James, Bill, Lloyd, Ralph, and Roger. But the women far outnumber us.)

There are several tree-named streets at the east end of the city: Alder, Aspen, Larch, Birch, Spruce, Cedar, Pine, and Willow. Not to mention the nearby Forest Avenue and Woods Avenue.

Miscellaneous Other Street Names in Storey County

Geiger Grade (State Route 341, Comstock Highway)

Named after Davison M. Geiger, the area physician who originally financed its construction. Originally, the route was a toll road between Virginia City and Steamboat Springs; later, though, the state took it over, then replaced it with a paved highway in 1936. Parts of the original road still exist (hence, Toll Road at the bottom of the grade), but no actual tolls are involved to get up the hill to Virginia City nowadays.

The Geiger route was one of many toll roads in the area. It seemed as though those who wanted to mine did so; but for those who wanted to make money from mining indirectly, the way to do so was to build a road the miners had to pass along. But toll roads were not all bad, as the toll road owners had to pay a tax on their income, and that tax went to build schools all over the Comstock.

Mark Twain, on Toll Roads

The legislature sat sixty days, and passed private toll-road franchises all the time. When they adjourned it was estimated that every citizen owned about three franchises, and it was believed that unless Congress gave the Territory another degree of longitude there would not be room enough to accommodate the toll-roads. The ends of them were hanging over the boundary line everywhere like a fringe.

The fact is, the freighting business has grown to such important proportions that there was nearly as much excitement over suddenly acquired toll-road fortunes as over the wonderful silver mines.

(Mark Twain, *Roughing It*, 1873.)

Lousetown Road

Named for the old mining camp to which the road once led.

There has been discussion for decades of someday improving this road and turning it into part of the state highway system. A highway would run from the county seat at Virginia City to the Derby Dam area of northern Storey County, which would eliminate the need for residents of that area to travel through the Reno-Sparks area to take care of county business. Such a plan is first discussed in the *Reno Evening Gazette* as far back as 1931, but generations later it is still a quiet, isolated road leading to a small housing development.

French street names in Lockwood

These uniquely named streets were named in the early 1990s,

when the Rainbow Bend area was first platted. One of the developers, Linda Hoy, was insistent that there be door-to-door mail delivery at individual mailboxes, rather than the cluster mailboxes that had started to become the norm in newer neighborhoods. The folks at the Sparks Post Office (which serves the Lockwood area) agreed, as long as there were no street names in the new community which were anything close to names already used in Reno or Sparks.

"Do you know how hard that is?" Hoy recollected. "But since I would sometimes see rainbows along the river, I wanted a color theme. I decided to name them after the French names for different colors. I grabbed a dictionary and went to work. *Voila.*"

Sometime later, someone actually visiting from France pointed out the error in one of the street names ("Divoire" should be "D'Ivoire") but the error was never corrected. Nonetheless, the French names remain as a testament to the individuality of the small community east of Sparks, and their residents still get mail from individual mailboxes.

SOURCES

Barber, Alicia. *Reno's Big Gamble: Image and Reputation in the Biggest Little City*. Lawrence, Kansas: University Press of Kansas, 2008.

Bath, Alison. "For nearly a century, Gasparis have been a part of Spanish Springs." *Reno Gazette-Journal*, June 17, 2003.

Bonner, T.D. *The Life and Adventures of James P. Beckwourth, Mountaineer, Scout, and Pioneer, and Chief of the Crow Nation of Indians, Written from his own Dictation*. New York: Harper and Brothers, 1856.

Breckenridge, Karl. *You're Doing WHAT to the Mapes?* Reno, Nevada: Jack Bacon and Company. 2005.

Breckenridge, Karl. "Readers' complaints about 'cold' subjects leads to warmer topic of pools; Reno Nostalgia" *Reno Gazette-Journal*, January 28, 2007

Breckenridge, Karl. "A Pocket Full of Notes." *Reno Gazette-Journal*, October 15, 2005.

Breckenridge, Karl. "A Saturday Morning Chism Sundae." *Reno Gazette-Journal*, February 26, 2005.

Brown, George Rothwell, ed. *Reminiscences of Senator William J. Stewart of Nevada*. New York: Neale Publishing Company, 1908.

Browne, J. Ross. "A Peep at Washoe." *Harper's Magazine*, December 1860.

Browne, J. Ross. "Washoe Revisited." *Harper's Magazine*, May 1865.

Bullis, Rose M. *History of the Washoe County Schools 1857-1912*. Sparks, Nevada: Western Printing and Publishing, 1979.

Carlson, Helen S. *Nevada Place Names: A Geographical Dictionary*. Reno, Nevada: University of Nevada Press, 1974.

Cerveri, Doris. *With Curry's Compliments: The Story of Abraham Curry*. Elko: Nostalgia Press, 1990.

Chism, Gordon H. *As I Remember: The Clark-Chism Family*. Mendocino, CA: 2004.

Cladianos, Pete Jr. *My Father's Son: A Gaming Memoir*. Reno, Nevada: University of Nevada Oral History Program, 2002.

Clifton, Guy. "Angela Dandini Dies at 88." *Reno Gazette-Journal*, October 17, 2003.

Clifton, Guy, "Center gives youths a place to relax, socialize." *Reno Gazette-Journal*, March 14, 2008.

Cofone, Albin. "Reno's Little Italy: Italian Entrepreneurship and Culture in Northern Nevada." *Nevada Historical Society Quarterly*, Summer 1983., 1913-1918." Nevada Historical Society Quarterly, Winter 1975.

Curtis, Donnelyn. *Historic Photos of Reno*. Nashville: Turner Publishing, 2008.

Dromiack, C. "Model Dairy Founder Recalls Early Day Distribution Problems; C.W. Brooks Reflects as New Plant Costing $250,000 Opens" *Reno Evening Gazette*, December 9, 1961.

Duggan, Brian. "Northgate closer to becoming a park." *Reno Gazette-Journal*, July 25, 2011

Edwards, Jerome. "Nevada's Power Broker: Pat McCarran and his Political Machine," *Nevada Historical Society Quarterly*, Winter 1975. http://nsla.nevadaculture.org/statepubs/epubs/210777-1975-4Winter.pdf

Edwards, Jerome. "Patrick A. McCarran: His Years on the Nevada Supreme Court." *Nevada Historical Society Quarterly*, Fall 1984.

Elliott, Gary E. *Senator Alan Bible and the Politics of the New West*. Reno: University of Nevada Press, 1994.

Gerould, Katharine Fullerton. "Reno." *Harper's Magazine*, June 1925.

Hammon, Amanda. "Fuji Park is actually Carson City Fairgrounds." *Nevada Appeal*, December 31, 1999.

Harber, Terry. "Fourth-generation Nevadan dies at 97." *Nevada Appeal*, April 3, 2007.

Harber, Terry. "Park planned for north end near design stage." *Nevada Appeal*, July 31, 2006.

Harber, Terry. "Residents asked to suggest names for park in Silver Oak." *Nevada Appeal*, April 9, 2007.

Heller, Linda. "Trip up old Kingsbury is ride down Memory Lane." *Record-Courier*, July 22, 2000.

Historic Reno Preservation Society. *A Walk Through Time: The Historic Powning's Addition in Reno*, Nevada. Reno, Nevada: Historic Reno Preservation Society, 2004.

Hixman, Dan. "Caddie Recalls Reno's Early Golf Days." *Reno Gazette-Journal*, June 5, 2006, Available online at http://gotorenotahoe.com/news/stories/html/2006/06/05/2389.php

Howard, Thomas Frederick. *Sierra Crossing: First Roads to California*. Berkeley, California: University of California Press, 1998.

Hoy, Linda. Personal discussion in her office in Lockwood, Nevada. February 25, 2013.

Hulse, James W. *The Silver State*. Reno, Nevada: University of Nevada Press, 1998.

Keegan, Roseann. "What's In A Name? Rich History behind well-known Tahoe spots." *Tahoe Daily Tribune*, July 3, 2010.

Kling, Dwayne. *The Rise of the Biggest Little City: An Encyclopedic History of Reno Gaming*, 1931-1981. Reno, Nevada: University of Nevada Press, 2000.

Land, Barbara and Myrick. *Reno: A Short History*. Reno, Nevada: University of Nevada Press, 1995.

Las Vegas Sun. "Family opposes parole of convicted killer." January 10, 1997.

Legislative Council Bureau, Research Division, Nevada Legislators 1861-2011. April 2011.

Lekisch, Barbara. *Tahoe Place Names: The origin and history of names in the Lake Tahoe Basin.* Lafayette, CA: Great West Books, 1988.

Lopez-Bowlan, Ellie. "NHS: 30 years of work for Hispanics." *Reno Gazette-Journal*, May 5, 2005.

Los Angeles Times. "Two Plead Guilty to Electrocuting Former Councilman in Nevada Town for $40,000." July 26, 1987.

Lyman, George D. *Ralston's Ring*. New York: Charlie Scribner's Sons, 1937.

McAndrew, Siobhan. "Bowling With Beasley: Thousands have knocked down pins, with Nellie leading the way." *Reno Gazette-Journal*, March 30, 2007.

McNair-Mathews, Mary. *Ten Years in Nevada, or Life on the Pacific Coast.* Originally published 1880 by Baker, Jones. Reprinted 1985 University of Nebraska Press.

Miller, Joaquin. "Horace Greeley Crossing the Sierras." *Sacramento Daily Record-Union*, December 24, 1887.

Moreno, Richard. *A Short History of Carson City*. Reno: University of Nevada Press, 2011.

Morrow, Sue. "Revered Music Director Al Saliman deserves correct pronunciation." *Nevada Appeal*, November 2, 2010.

Myers, Dennis. "Highway Blues." *Reno News and Review*, July 6, 2006.

Myles, Myrtle. *Nevada Governors: From Territorial Days to the Present.* Sparks, NV: Western Printing and Publishing, 1972.

Nevada Appeal. "A Story that should live on in Nevada history." April 8, 2007.

Nevada Evening Gazette, "Another School is Opened—Another Teacher Honored." December 1, 1957

Nevada State Journal, "Children Will Have Playground: Council Plans to Repair Riverside Park and Construct New Driveway." March 28, 1914

Nevada State Journal, "Employes' Donation Praised." August 23, 1968.

Nevada State Journal, "Home Gardens Merger Plan is Delayed: Annexation Hearing Draws Heated Arguments," September 10, 1947.

Nevada State Journal, "Hospital Park Named to Honor Samuel Pickett." March

21, 1947.

Nevada State Journal, "Kuenzli Street Dedication Set." February 28, 1952.

Nevada State Journal, "Mr. Gerow [sic] Wants to Reciprocate in Naming of Streets." January 16, 1952.

Nevada State Journal, "New Sparks Junior High Honors Nevada Educator." May 14, 1961.

Nevada State Journal, "Overpass Dedication Set February 9." January 29, 1970.

Nevada State Journal, "Six Street Names in Reno Due for Clarification: Planning Commission Assumes Task of Christening." April 22, 1954.

Nevada State Journal, "Two Washoe Schools Named in Honor of Veteran Nevada Educators By County Board." April 13, 1957.

Nicoletta, Julie. *Buildings of Nevada*. Chicago: Oxford University Press, 2000.

Nielson, Norm. *Reno: The Past Revisited*. Norfolk, Virginia: The Donning Company, 1988.

O'Driscoll, Pat. "Reno's Old Mt. Rose School To Be Closed in June." *Reno Evening Gazette*, February 23, 1977.

Paher, Stanley, ed. *Nevada: Official Bicentennial Book*. Las Vegas, Nevada: Nevada Publications, 1976.

Peckham, George R. "Reminiscences of An Active Life," circa 1920. From the collection of the Nevada State Historical Society. Available online at http://www.library.unlv.edu/boomtown/nhsp/nhsp_v2.pdf

Phillips, Bill. "Gomes Gets Good Marks as Freshman Legislator," *Nevada State Journal*, March 27, 1977.

Prouty, Annie E. "The Development of Reno in Relation to its Topography." *Nevada State Historical Society Papers*, Vol. IV 1923-1924, pp. 29-189.

Pryor, Alton. *Little Known Tales in Nevada History*. Roseville, California: Stagecoach Publishing, 2003.

Raymond, C. Elizabeth. *George Wingfield: Owner and Operator of Nevada*. Reno: University of Nevada Press, 1992.

Reno Evening Gazette, "26 Elementary Schools Open Doors Sept. 3," August 27, 1957

Reno Evening Gazette, "After Prayers, Speeches, It's Fishing Time," September 30, 1964

Reno Evening Gazette, "Ethel Zimmer, Native of Franktown, Dies." December 8, 1960.

Reno Evening Gazette, "No Bar Found to Park Site for Library." September 27, 1962.

Reno Evening Gazette, "Reno to Buy Land for City Park," September 1, 1964.

Reno Evening Gazette. "Legislators Plan to Offer Bills Next Week." January 23, 1931

Reno Gazette-Journal, "Honoring Jesse Hall." February 7, 2006.

Reno Gazette-Journal, "People who helped make Sparks what it is today." June 10, 2005

Reno Gazette-Journal, "Wedekinds found Silver, Gold, Zinc Deposits." May 18, 2004.

Roccapriore, Carla. "School Naming Panel to Meet." *Reno Gazette-Journal,* October 17, 2004.

Rocha, Guy. "Forgotten Paternity of Carson." *Nevada Appeal,* February 24, 2008.

Rocha, Guy. "Carson's Founders Give Way to New Generation." *Nevada Appeal,* March 23, 2008.

Shipley, Jarid. "Poor Residents Used to be Kept at Farm." *Nevada Appeal,* May 28, 2006.

Smith, Barry. "Not enough streets, too many names." *Nevada Appeal,* November 21, 2003.

Sparks Centennial History Committee, *History of Sparks: Centennial Edition.* 2004.

Sutro, Adolph. *The Mineral Resources of the United States,.* Baltimore: Murphy and Company, 1868. (Available for download at http://books.google.com/books?id=oNUOAAAAYAAJ)

Thompson and West, Publishers. *History of Nevada With Illustrations and Biographical Sketches of its Prominent Men and Pioneers.* Oakland, CA: Thompson and West, 1881.

Townley, Carrie M. "Bishop Whitaker's School for Girls." *Nevada Historical Society Quarterly,* Fall 1976.

Townley, John M. *Tough Little Town on the Truckee: Reno 1868-1900.* Reno, Nevada: Great Basin Studies Center, 1983.

Voyles, Susan. "Activist McAlinden, 87, 'a real fighter' for Stead." *Reno Gazette-Journal,* April 17, 2003.

Voyles, Susan. "A New Era for the Truckee." *Reno Gazette-Journal,* November 3, 2003.

Voyles, Susan, "Potholes Plague Private Road." *Reno Gazette-Journal,* February 25, 2005.

Voyles, Susan, "River Inn land up for sale, lease." *Reno Gazette-Journal,* April 3, 2007.

Walton-Buchanan, Holly. *Historic Houses and Buildings of Reno, Nevada.* Reno, Nevada: Black Rock Press, 2007.

Wellem, Bel. "Remembering the woman, Yvonne Shaw." *Reno Gazette-Journal,* August 10, 2004.

Whited, Fred E., Jr. "Senator Patrick A. McCarran: Orator from Nevada."

Nevada Historical Society Quarterly, Winter 1974, pp. 181-202.

Wier, Jeanne E. (ed.) *Nevada Historical Society Papers 1917-1920*. Reno: A. Carlisle and Co., 1920.

Willem, Bel. "The rule is there are no rules to naming streets around Sparks." *Reno Gazette-Journal*, February 24, 2004.

Woodmansee, Karen. "All toll roads led to the Comstock – almost: The Six Mile Canyon Route was a free road." *Nevada Appeal*, July 9, 2006.

Zauner, Phyllis and Lou. *Reno-Sparks Nevada: A Mini-History*. Tahoe Paradise, CA: Zanel Publications, 1978.

Zimmer, Ethel. "Key Role Played by Haskell." *Nevada State Journal*, June 19, 1960.

Zimmer, Ethel. "Marsh Avenue Honors Rancher." *Nevada State Journal*, July 17, 1960.

Zimmer, Ethel. "Morrill Avenue Honors Builder." *Nevada State Journal*, May 29, 1960.

Zimmer, Ethel. "2 Thoroughfares Named for Pioneer." *Nevada State Journal*, May 22, 1960.

Zimmer, Ethel. "Reno's Wheeler Avenue Named for Prominent Local Rancher." *Nevada State Journal*, July 31, 1960.

Zimmer, Ethel. "Ryland's Name From Real Estate Man." *Nevada State Journal*, March 27, 1960.

Web sites of interest:

The First 100 Persons Who Shaped Southern Nevada, http://www.1st100.com/

James Pierson Beckwourth, http://www.beckwourth.org/

Chism House History, http://www.chismhouse.com/history.php

Corrigan's Way: Right or Wrong, He Made His Mark on History (by Stan Sears), http://www.airportjournals.com/Display.cfm?varID=0503005

DRI Honors Senator Raggio and KOLO News 8 With President's Medal, http://www.dri.edu/news/news-release-archives/2629-dri-honors-senator-raggio-and-kolo-news-channel-8-with-presidents-medal

Finding Forgotten Empire City – Rick Moreno, http://backyardtraveler.blogspot.com/2009/01/finding-forgotten-empire-city.html

Flood Chronology of the Carson River Basin, California and Nevada, http://nevada.usgs.gov/crfld/data_byflood_17_reach2.cfm

Historic California Posts: Post at Friday's Station, http://www.militarymuseum.org/FridaysSta.html

Historical Myth a Month: Facing the Truth about some of our Best but Tallest Tales, http://nsla.nevadaculture.org/index.php?option=com_content&view=article&id=683&Itemid=440

History of Robert Mitchell Elementary School, http://www.robertmitchell

elementary.com/history-of-school.html

Isbell Family Genealogy Forum, http://genforum.genealogy.com/isbell/messages/305.html

Italian American Innovators, http://www.care2.com/c2c/groups/disc.html?gpp=6454&pst=274776\

The Man Who Invented the Wheel, and Paid the Price (by Dennis Bell), http://freepages.genealogy.rootsweb.ancestry.com/~wanda/ferriswheel.html

Museum of Gaming History, http://museumofgaminghistory.org/mogh_home.php

Nevada History in Maps, http://www.delamare.unr.edu/maps/digitalcollections/nvhistory/

Nevada State Legislators: Historical Information, http://www.leg.state.nv.us/dbtw-wpd/LegSim.htm

Nevada Women's History Project, http://www.unr.edu/nwhp/

The PFE Icehouse, A History by Karl Breckenridge, http://www.karlbreckenridge.com/pfe_icehouse.htm

Park Family—115 Years of History at Lake Tahoe, http://www.laketahoenews.net/2011/06/park-family-115-years-of-history-at-lake-tahoe/

Pioneer Days in Sparks and Vicinity as viewed by F.B. Kingsbury in 1924, http://www.nevadaobserver.com/Reading Room Documents/Pioneer Days in Sparks and Vicinity (1924).htm

Saint Theresa of Lisieux Parish, South Lake Tahoe, History, http://www.sainttheresachurch.org/framehistory.html

Spooner Summit: Nevada Historical Marker 261, http://nvshpo.org/index.php?option=com_content&task=view&id=214 &Itemid=9

Stead Training Center Historical Information, http://www.globalsecurity.org/military/facility/stead.htm

Adolph Sutro: A Biography by the Virtual Museum of the City of San Francisco http://www.sfmuseum.net/sutro/bio.html

Carson City's Historic Personalities, http://www.carson-city.org/history/personalities.php

Moana Hot Springs: Geological Survey, http://www.nbmg.unr.edu/geothermal/site.php?sid=moana%20hot%20springs

Nevada History by John C. Evanoff, http://visitreno.com/evanoff/index.php

Nevada's Radio History. http://www.radioblvd.com/nevradiohist.htm

Overview of the History of the Reno Lodge, http://renoelks.org/history.html

LaVere Redfield Remembered, http://www.renocoinclub.org/Redfield.html

Library of Congress: Empire City Photo, http://www.loc.gov/pictures/

item/2002723869/

Guy Rocha's Historical Myth A Month, http://nevadaculture.org/nsla/index.php? option=com_content&task=view&id=683&Itemid=97

Steamboat Hot Springs (A history by John C. Evanoff), http://www.visitreno. com/ evanoff/jan-09.php

Mark Twain Quotations, Newspaper Collections, & Related Resources, http://www.twainquotes.com/index.html

Washoe County Board of County Commissioners: Staff Report on the Future of Northgate Golf Course, http://www.co.washoe.nv.us/large_files/ agendas/030309/8.pdf

West of Wells Neighborhood Group and Bungalow District, http://www. westofwells.com/

ABOUT THE AUTHOR

James D. Umbach moved to Reno from California in 2005. He has a degree in Government from California State University, Sacramento, but is interested in just about everything. He is a bellman at John Ascuaga's Nugget in Sparks, where he enjoys interacting with guests and using his knowledge of the area to help enhance the guest experience. He was a member of the Washoe County Library Board of Trustees and visits the library frequently.

When he is not working, reading, or writing, his interests include hiking, camping, and visiting new places around Nevada and California.

He has been married to his wife, Dione, since 2005.

Author's Note

Do you have comments, questions, or general feedback? I would love to hear from you! You can write me at james@renostreetnames.com or find me on Facebook: www.facebook.com/james.umbach.

And while you're on the Internet, check out this book's website at www.renostreetnames.com for lots of cool extras, photos, and fun stuff!

CPSIA information can be obtained at www.ICGtesting.com
Printed in the USA
BVOW02s0057130913

331037BV00002B/30/P